ON THE JOB

The Christian
9 to 5

Sharon Coursey

ON THE JOB

The Christian 9 to 5

Sir Fred Catherwood

Edited by George N. Monsma, Jr.

ZONDERVAN PUBLISHING HOUSE OF THE ZONDERVAN CORPORATION GRAND RAPIDS, MICHIGAN 49506

ON THE JOB: THE CHRISTIAN 9 TO 5
Published in Great Britain under the title *The Christian in Industrial Society*

Published by special arrangement with Inter-Varsity Press,
38 De Montfort Street,
Leicester LEI 7GP, England.

Library of Congress Cataloging in Publication Data

Catherwood, H. F. R. (Henry Frederick Ross), Sir, 1925-
On the job.

Previously published under title: The Christian in industrial society.
Includes index.
1. Church and labor. I. Monsma, George N. II. Title.
HD6338.C244 1983 261.8'5 82-23716
ISBN 0-310-37261-5

Designed by Louise Bauer and James E. Ruark

Printed in the United States of America

83 84 85 86 87 88 / 10 9 8 7 6 5 4 3 2 1

Contents

Publisher's Preface

ALTHOUGH IN THE course of working and reading the daily newspaper one is more likely to think of the gulf that geographically separates the United States from Western Europe—if one considers the matter at all—there is much more in common economically and culturally than our own disinterest suggests. It is therefore with a sense of gratitude for British foresight and a vision for the future that we publish this book. *On the Job* provides a keen glimpse and timely discussion of the common problems, achievements, and challenges that confront the Western World. The similarities between the nations that straddle the Atlantic loom much greater and more significant than the differences.

Because there are differences, however, not only in economics and culture but also in language, we commend George N. Monsma, Jr., for his editorial assistance. Dr. Monsma, who holds the M.A. and Ph.D. degrees from Princeton University, is Professor of Economics at Calvin College, Grand Rapids, Michigan, and is a Fellow of the Calvin Center for Christian Scholarship. His research, insight, and understanding have proved invaluable in making this book highly readable and applicable to its readers in the United States.

We are grateful also to the author and to Inter-Varsity Press for their assistance and cooperation in our revising their book for this American edition.

Preface to the Third Edition

SINCE THIS BOOK was first published in 1964, it has sold 30,000 copies; it continues to be in demand and its ideas seem to have stood the test of time. But the industrial scene has changed dramatically with new and intractable problems.

Not all the trends are bad. There is a new and welcome concern for the poverty of the third world. But corruption has become more blatant, and companies and governments have had to acknowledge it and to take public positions. In Europe progressive taxation and inflation combined to reduce reward for risk and effort and have produced a "black economy." E. F. Schumacher's *Small Is Beautiful* has attacked the economics of scale and especially the inbred assumptions of the big nationalized monopoly whose scientists lay down the line that divides what is safe and unsafe. Ralph Nader's *Unsafe at Any Speed* has made the same challenge to private industry. The "Club of Rome" has asked whether we have the resources for perpetual economic growth, a question almost immediately underlined by the first oil crisis following the Yom Kippur war in 1973 and brought home even more dramatically by the widespread oil shortage of 1979. Environmentalists have sprung from nowhere to question the basic assumptions of industrial society. But more intractable than any of these problems has been the rise of cost-push inflation wrecking the benign postwar Keynesian economic expansion, which had produced the greatest increase in real wealth in the history of the world. Now the stable currencies of the Bretton Woods agreement are a memory and the economic growth that gave full employment to industrialized countries and hope to the rest of the world seems to be a forgotten dream.

In 1964, in the flood tide of economic expansion, the problems in the book were put a little apologetically and the warnings given then now read a good deal more tentatively than we would put them today. The Christian world has changed too. In 1964 the reaction against the "social gospel" was still strong, and comment on social affairs was left to the liberal wing of the church. Evangelicals had forgotten the traditions of Wilberforce and Shaftesbury. Evangelism and personal piety were the twin goals. The Catholic hierarchy seemed to treat poverty as an act of God. This book broke new ground. Now that social commitment has become fashionable, the pendulum has swung over, and those of us who had to fight the battle for social commitment sometimes feel entitled to remind today's generation of the terms of the argument. We tried to show that the Christians should bring their social and political assumptions to the bar of God's Word; otherwise we are infiltrated by the worldly assumptions of our time, which we cover with a thin veneer of Christianity. There may be a great deal of good in some of the new secular causes Christians have now rushed to join, but they are not all Christian causes, and we need to bring them too to the bar of a truly Christian judgment.

Today's danger is the old one all over again: Are we judging an issue on current political assumptions? Is our judgment any different from that of the good humanist? Christian assumptions are different from those of the liberal humanist and the secular conservative, the Marxist and the socialist. The church must judge the *Zeitgeist* by Christian assumptions. The rock of truth stands over against the tides of worldly opinion.

Finally, the author has gained a great deal more experience of the world with long spells in public service to complement the experience in industry. Just as the experience as a chief executive of public companies had concentrated the mind in what had to be done and what could be done, so the experience in public service has helped in understanding the objects and constraints of governments and labor unions. And four years spent in promoting British trade around the world helped to underline the vast difference between the cultures and assumptions of different countries and their governments. Although Christian principles never change, it helps, in our understanding of their application to the world in which we live, to have some firsthand experiences of the real pressures on governments, on organizations, and on people. And yet it is not the Christian's duty to accept these pressures. We must maintain our own ideals, give a vision of the better society that Christian ideals might achieve, and give methods of achieving those ideals that are practical and therefore credible.

I hope this revision makes some contribution to the new and dangerous problems we all now face.

Preface to the First and Second Editions

THIS BOOK CAME into being as a result of a series of discussions between a dozen Christians directly concerned with industry and commerce. Each discussion was based on a paper by a member and the book is based on the papers, the conclusions of the resultant discussions, and also the further discussion resulting from the publication of some of the findings in *The Christian Graduate*. What is written is not based on the view or experience of one individual. On the other hand, it was felt best that one person should draw the threads together and that it was neither necessary nor desirable to have everyone in the group in agreement with every conclusion in the book.

The main concern of this book is in setting standards for the Christian by applying Christian doctrine to behavior in society today. But there are also some ways of organizing society itself that are unquestionably helpful to the maintenance of Christian standards and others that are not. We felt that it would be most useful to take two or three chapters to set out the points at issue. In a few key questions we have gone a little further and set out some solutions, not because we felt that they were the only solutions for a Christian, but because we felt the necessity of showing that Christian principles could, in fact, be worked out in a practical way and should not be dismissed as visionary or impractical.

The last chapters of the book deal with our relations with people, those with whom we trade, our employers, our employees and colleagues, and with the particular problems a Christian faces in working in a society that does not hold strictly to the standards of his own faith.

We have found a remarkable absence of previous study on the subject, and if some conclusions appear to be unsupported or even dogmatic, we can only plead the absence of support, opposition, or dogma. To this extent we have had to rely on the experience of the group. We had a fairly wide range of experience and the members of the group held the kind of jobs in which people have to make up their own minds about the problems under discussion.

Although everyone in the group has taken a great deal of time and trouble in preparing papers, in discussion, and in comments on the drafts, special thanks are due to Dr. Oliver Barclay, who went through each draft chapter in detail, commenting, amending, and in places, rewriting. Thanks are also due to the editor of *The Christian Graduate* for permission to reprint chapters 1–4, which originally appeared as articles in that magazine, September 1962 to June 1963; to my wife for her work in making the text lucid; and to Mary Agnew for arranging the meetings and for typing the drafts in addition to a full day in her ordinary job. I must also, on my own behalf, thank my wife for her help and also for her forbearance in looking after three small children alone on the holidays and Saturdays during which this book was written.

—Sir Fred Catherwood

ON THE JOB

The Christian
9 to 5

Introduction

THERE WOULD HARDLY be any argument today against the view that the Christian church has a diminishing impact on society. The church itself does not bother to dispute the point. Its time and attention are taken up with the means of re-establishing the contact it appears to have lost. The remedies vary according to the theological position of their exponents. There are those who see their strength in the authority of age-old ritual. Others, in the hope of keeping the church in fashion, are prepared to make almost every conceivable concession to contemporary philosophy until what is left is unrecognizable as Christianity. Others see the ecumenical movement as the basis of a restored authority. Still others continue to preach the "social gospel," trying to apply the teaching of our Lord to His disciples directly to unregenerate society as if there were no need for personal repentance and forgiveness.

Evangelicals for too long concentrated almost exclusively on personal evangelism, believing that nothing can be achieved without personal regeneration, and were prepared to evangelize in complete independence of the church if they were not free to work within it. As the state of the church grew more desperate, evangelicals felt increasingly compelled toward this policy. There seemed to be no time for anything but insistence on the key doctrines of personal regeneration and faith. That has now changed, and the doctrine that Christians are the salt of the earth is much more widely accepted.

While there was still a considerable collective impact by Christians in society and while social behavior was strongly influenced by Christian standards, the old evangelical emphasis gave a proper balance. It is now open to question whether the balance is still there, and whether Christians should not make a collective impact on society.

It is true that, according to the New Testament accounts, personal evangelism was the order of the day in the early church. But it was done by individual Christians and by a church whose philosophy and behavior were both coherent and visibly different from those of the pagan world around.

The Christian testimony to the truth is by both life and word. In practice the testimony of our lives precedes and provides the occasion for the testimony of our message. The emphasis of the Epistles is overwhelmingly on what we should do rather than on what we should say. People are likely to listen if the sort of life we lead makes them think that there is something worth listening to.

The witness of the individual in word and deed has its place, but it is remarkable how much emphasis there is also on collective witness. That the Corinthian church should condone immoral behavior is as serious to Paul as the immoral behavior itself. The witness of the Holy Spirit at Pentecost was through all the church together. Individuals may be written off as cranks. It is not so easy to write off a lively and active church with old and young, men and women, rich and poor, dull and bright, introvert and extrovert, new converts and long-established Christians. It demonstrates that the Christian faith is not just for the individual on his own, but is a way of life affecting people in all their relations with one another. Can we neglect these social implications of Christianity altogether without disobedience to New Testament teaching? If we do so, are we not likely to withdraw into Sunday religion and parlor Christianity, which will not even begin to touch the world around?

This book is written out of the conviction that although the primary responsibility of the church is to believe and to spread the gospel, it is also essential and not merely optional to try to see how we should obey God in daily life. For all engaged in commerce and industry, particularly in the new and complicated institutions of modern life, this involves special problems. But in solving these problems it also gives the opportunity to set standards for future generations, as past generations of Christians have set standards for us. In this book we shall try to see what obedience to Christian teaching means in some major aspects of industrial society as we know it today.

It is our conviction that the Bible does teach that God cares about the social order. Righteousness, justice, love for the weak, and other virtues are not only to be practiced in private but, as we are taught in Romans 13, should be a feature of society. But the establishment of codes of social righteousness will not of itself lead anyone into the Christian faith. To concentrate on this to the exclusion of all else is not to preach a balanced gospel either. People must know what demands

God makes on them, but they must realize that these demands are individual before they are collective; they must know the results of disobedience and the way of salvation.

There is, therefore, no "social *gospel.*" The gospel is addressed to the individual. Society collectively cannot be redeemed. It can, however, be reformed according to the law of God. There is a "social *law.*" Society in any of its sectors can be made more or less righteous, and Christians must be concerned that, as far as they are able to accomplish it, righteousness shall prevail in those spheres in which they are involved, whether it is a school, a local government, or a business. To leave them to secularism or humanism would be a complete abdication of our responsibility as Christian citizens.

The preaching and teaching of God's law has two functions. First, it is "our schoolmaster to bring us to Christ." It is an essential background to evangelism. Repentance precedes salvation, and conviction of sin precedes repentance. The first object of the preacher must be to bring home to people that God's standards are not their standards, and he must do this in terms of the kind of life that they lead, the kind of standards they set, and the kind of temptations to which they are prone. Industrial society brings new temptations and requires the setting of new standards. The rural pastor understood the *mores* of rural society. It is questionable whether the suburban minister has nearly the same close knowledge of what his congregation are up to during the week. Their behavior on Sunday may be no indication whatever of their relation to their fellows in the anonymity of the big city or within the closed society of the great corporation. God's law should be made to apply as much in the one place as in the other.

To disagree with the social gospeler's idea that society could be redeemed collectively through good works does not necessarily mean that there is no purpose in applying the moral law to the unbeliever. We may not expect the moral law to produce a society of Christians, but by the preaching of Christian standards and by the work of God's grace we can expect a better society.

The children of Israel were instructed by both the law and the prophets as to the precise temptations of an agricultural society and their proper behavior to each other and to strangers. Our Lord does not hesitate to instruct His disciples on their attitude toward money, taxation, and their foreign rulers; and Peter, Paul and James in their epistles are all concerned with the detailed problems arising from life in a pagan society. Who are we, in our day, to feel that we have no need for such things? And if our Lord was concerned with the earthly needs and sufferings of the society in which He lived, who are we to be indifferent?

The other function of the law is as a means of "common grace." This is the grace given by God to the church and the world alike. God has not given the world over to evil. Even where there is no Christian church and no Christian witness, good is still preserved. The Christian is not yet in heaven, nor is the man of the world in hell. God is still present. His influence is still felt. His Spirit still strives with man. He works through conscience, through the divine institutions of government and family, and perhaps most forcibly of all through the explicit proclamation of God's law by the church.

Occasionally God has withdrawn this preserving grace. We read of it in the stories of the Flood and of Sodom, and in the first chapter of Paul's Epistle to the Romans. It may be, too, that this is what happened to Jerusalem before it was razed by Titus. God took Noah and Lot away from the society in which each was involved. He warned the church that the time must come for them to leave Jerusalem to its fate. But while they were there, they were to proclaim God's law; and while we are here, we too must continue to proclaim God's law and make our contribution to the preservation of the society in which we live.

We are not, as we explain later in the book, expecting to set out a blueprint for a specifically Christian society or company. Indeed it is not at all clear what that would mean. We are concerned to try to explore ways in which explicit biblical teaching and general Christian values work out in these spheres, and how this section of the contemporary world could be made to conform more closely to these Christian ideals.

NEW SOCIAL PATTERNS

For society has changed out of all recognition since Christianity attained its last peak of power and influence about a hundred years ago. It has changed radically even since the present pattern of theological positions, parties, and movements became established round about the turn of the century. The old social pattern centered around the local community. Half the population a century ago was still agricultural, and even the industrial population of a particular town would have been, for the most part, more stable than it is today. More likely than not, people would have lived in the same surroundings and among the same neighbors for most of their lives. Today, the majority of the population of Britain are townspeople, and of these the majority live in huge, impersonal conurbations, whose millions scarcely know their neighbors or their workmates. They may change their neighborhood a number of times in a lifetime and their job a good deal more often. This is the age of a society that is increasingly nomadic and atomized and where even the basic unity of society, the family, is in increasing danger of being split up. There have been many instruments of this change, but the greatest single cause must surely be the power of industrialization that has loosened the narrow confines of traditional society.

Christians cannot disregard these changes. We must set new guidelines, and to do this we must make some judgment on the forces which shape society. This is what Christians have always tried to do in periods of strength and vigor. We cannot limit our views to behavior on Sunday and in the home. The Reformers took no limited or half-hearted view of society. We cannot imagine an Augustine, a Luther, a Calvin, a Knox, a Wilberforce, or a Shaftesbury living in our day and declining to express a view on the right and wrong behavior in the kind of world in which they had to live. To each of these men, there was no problem of morals and behavior that was beyond the competence of God's Word. They would not have understood the idea that some mysterious and unalterable economic law somehow overrode a Christian's clearly taught obligations to his neighbor. It is wrong to water down the message of sin, judgment, and redemption to a "do good" social gospel. But it is also wrong to preach as if God's Word is not relevant to men's relations to their fellows, that is, to society as we find it.

Those who are always demanding that the church pronounce on this or that may find this argument somewhat unnecessary, but in this theologically confused generation there can be no harm in a little definition of one's position.

It should be emphasized that this is not a political pamphlet. This is a book to help Christians apply the principles of their faith in the society in which they live. It therefore assumes adherence to those principles. It does not presume to tell the humanist or the Jew how to apply his principles. It supposes that those whose faith is different may have different principles and that their conclusions may well be different too. We do believe, however, that Christian principles are the right ones, and that so far as people adhere to them society will be better, and so far as they depart from them it will be worse.

It may be that many who read the book may feel that what it says is not specifically Christian, that most of what is advocated could have come just as easily from anyone of high morality, whether Christian or not. Certainly it is no part of our case that there is a different verse from the Bible to solve every different moral problem in a highly complex industrial society. Nor do we claim always to be different from traditional morality. If traditional morality gives the same answers as Christianity, then so much the better for traditional morality.

But Christians must be sure that their behavior is at least as good as that of traditional morality. Our Lord told His disciples that their righteousness must exceed the righteousness of the scribes and the Pharisees. In fact the morality of countries like Britain and the United States owe to Christianity much more than they will now acknowledge; a good deal of what is best in the moral code of British and American society has been the working out of Christian morality in practice. In particular, respect for the dignity and responsibility of the individual has been a feature of our society that stems directly from Christian teaching and has been worked out in terms of universal suffrage, universal education, and individual liberty. This view of the individual must therefore be part of any Christian view of industrial society. The purpose of this book is to work out the implications in industrial society of the Christian doctrines of the individual and of their social relationships, rather than to prove these doctrines all over again to people who substantially accept them.

Edward Norman, the speaker in 1978 for the British Broadcasting Corporation's annual Reith Lectures, made a strong attack on the politicization of Christianity. His target was the World Council of Churches and its growing insistence that the Christian church must take a position on one side or another in the major political issues of the day. He criticized the World Council for political bias and reminded us that the main task of the church is to preach the gospel in an evil world. Although he may have gone too far, many Christians felt that he had said what needed to be said and had redressed the balance. He has not been the only one to feel that the World Council of Churches has gone too far from a specifically Christian message. A few years ago a well-known bishop spent an afternoon in the chair at a WCC meeting while two younger prelates thundered on about imperialism. Finally something snapped, and he said, "Your generation have no experience of real imperialism. I was held for four years in a prison camp by your fellow countrymen. I do know what imperialism is, and it is not the main problem facing the Christian church today." He left the chair and the WCC, his ministry was transformed, and his tropical cathedral is now full of converts to the Christian faith.

But for every bishop with his care of souls, there are ten thousand

Christians whose main job is to tackle the problems of the world, who meet moral questions on the shop floor, on the stock exchange, in selling to customers and agents in countries with quite different business ethics. Decisions have to be made and moral judgments are needed. These judgments are not an optional extra; they are an integral part of everyday work in which a Christian is meant to live as a Christian and in which he is certainly judged as a Christian by his fellow workers. The Christian is in the world and cannot avoid its problems.

1 The Christian Attitude Toward Work

In the years following the Reformation it became apparent that there was an essential difference between the developing Protestant ethic and the preceding Catholic ethic in their attitudes toward work.[1] This in turn seemed to hinge on the difference in their respective attitudes toward the natural world around them. The Catholic tended to see the physical world as evil and to him the saint was one who had no part in it. The Catholic saint did not marry or trade. To him, spirituality came by physical withdrawal to holy ground—the monastery and the church—and by external rites. To the Protestant, the evil was within. As our Lord said, "The things which come out of man are what defile him."

The Protestant position was based on the nature of man as unfolded not only by our Lord, but throughout the Bible. The natural resources of the world were created by God and were given to man for his use. "Let us make man in our image, . . . and let them have dominion over the fish of the sea, and over the birds of the air, and over the cattle, and over all the earth" (Gen. 1:26). "And God blessed them, and God said to them, Be fruitful and multiply, and fill the earth and subdue it; and have dominion . . . over every living thing" (1:28). After the fall of man, the conditions are changed, but the objective is the same. "In the sweat of your face you shall eat bread" (3:19). The commission that was given to Adam was also given to Noah: "Be fruitful and multiply, and fill the earth. The fear of you and the dread of you shall be upon every beast of the earth, . . . into your hand they are delivered" (9:1–2).

We find the same thought in the psalms of David. "When I look at thy heavens, the work of thy fingers, the moon and the stars which thou hast established; what is man that thou art mindful of him?" He then goes on to answer his own question by setting out one of God's purposes

[1]See Appendix, "The Weber-Tawney Thesis."

for man on earth: "Thou hast given him dominion over the works of thy hands; thou hast put all things under his feet" (Ps. 8:3–4, 6). Man is a spiritual being, but he has been put on earth to fulfill the purposes of God, and one of these primary and basic purposes is that he should control and administer the natural resources of the world. He demonstrates the nature and purpose of God to those who do not believe by obedience to this basic commandment.

If a Christian is to be true to these principles, he does not work simply to make money or to pay the bills. He works because it is part of the divine order that he should work. Even Christian slaves had to remember this: "Slaves, obey in everything those who are your earthly masters, not with eye-service, as men-pleasers, but in singleness of heart, fearing the Lord" (Col. 3:22–23). Clearly, whatever our work is, we must do it with enthusiasm and not grudgingly or because we are driven to it. It appears to have come more naturally to the early Christians to evangelize than to work, and the exhortation to work is a constant refrain in Paul's epistles. "Aspire to live quietly, to mind your own affairs, and to work with your hands, as we charged you; so that you may command the respect of outsiders, and be dependent on nobody" (1 Thess. 4:11-12). Not only must a Christian work, he must work as if for God and he must work wholeheartedly. "Whatever your hand finds to do, do it with your might" (Eccl. 9:10). Our Lord's parable of the talents praises those who made maximum use of their resources and condemns the man who made no use of his because they were small.

It would be fair to deduce from this teaching that it is the duty of the Christian to use his abilities to the limit of his physical and mental capacity. He cannot relax as soon as he has enough money or as soon as he has mastered his job. He has a duty to train himself and develop his abilities, both academically and experimentally, to the limit that his other responsibilities allow. When he has mastered one job, he should go on to another. He should not be content to administer, but should try to improve and innovate. He should not stop until it is quite clear that he has reached his ceiling.

VALUES IN VOCATION

Christians who are not called to the ministry should ask, What is God's purpose in life for individual members of the Christian church? Is it to imitate on a smaller scale and part-time the work of the minister, or is it something separate and different? Too many people today seem to believe that the laity are without functions except those of ''personal evangelist'' and part-time preacher. But if we have gifts as evangelists and teachers, why should we not use them full-time? The teaching of the Bible on the function of the laity would appear to be much more positive. The church is here to glorify God before an unbelieving world by living the kind of life that God intended man to live. It must do what God intended man to do. It is clear from the passages quoted above that man was intended to control and put to use the untamed resources of the world. To this end he was given powers of intellect and organization. A Christian does not work to earn a living; he works because God intended that he should use the gifts he had given him for the fulfillment of a divine purpose. He goes on working whether or not he needs to earn a living. His work is a divine vocation and not to be treated lightly, whether he is a surgeon or a carpenter. No labor is degrading.

A servant with this clause
Makes drudgery divine:
Who sweeps a room, as for thy laws,
Makes that and the action fine.

Ultimately all of us must decide for ourselves on the limits beyond which we cannot stretch our physical and mental powers. We must decide too on the proportion of time and energy we must give to family and to spiritual devotions. This is a matter in which extremes are easy and a correct balance difficult. God has laid down that one day in seven should be devoted to Him, and we should go out of our way to see that no secular affairs spill over into that day. The family has a call on our energy and attention as well as our time, and no Christian has a right to allow his work to make his wife a widow or his children orphans.

It is not possible to achieve all these objectives at once without a fair degree of method and self-discipline. These are regarded today as rather old-fashioned virtues, and the modern world seems more concerned with a reduction of stress than with an increase in standards of service. The more complex our work and the less other people can see for themselves what we are doing and why, the more important it is that we should set our own standards. ''The professional must always determine himself what his work should be and what good work is. Neither what he should do, nor what standards should be applied, can be set for him'' (Peter Drucker, *The Practice of Management*). Christians, especially, must organize their life and work, must set their own high standards, and must examine the quality of their work continuously and critically against those standards.

It is also important that Christians should be able to recognize the symptoms of intellectual laziness and lack of self-control so that they can correct them whenever they appear. Someone who does his job in a lazy way loses his grip on the situation, and events take charge. Crises begin to arise, and he gets into a vicious circle of weariness and worry. In next to no time, he has used up his stock of emotional energy. Had he applied himself to his job in the first place, the situation would never have arisen.

Poor personal relationships usually come from lack of self-control and are another great cause of dissipation of emotional energy. There are, of course, people who are particularly difficult, fussy, and touchy, and we all have to work with them from time to time. But the person who is determined to control his antipathies and who refuses to let people get under his skin, who rides all personal misunderstandings lightly and refuses to take umbrage, will find that he has a good deal more energy left for his job than his more sensitive colleague. Yet nothing is a greater source of strength than a sense of competence, a feeling that you are on top of the situation and have the initiative. It is this that enables people not only to ride out the storm, but to have a sense of exhilaration in doing so. This sense of competence is not confined to Christians, but a Christian who does not feel it, and particularly a Christian who has allowed his job to "get on top of him," should examine the quality of his work to see whether he has been setting his standards and keeping to them as he ought.

PUTTING THE MIND TO WORK

The sloppy thinker will waste hours of his own and other people's time and energy in fruitless fussing. He is full of secondhand ideas and will run everything "the way we used to run it." His own ideas are usually half-baked. If he is in charge of others, he will keep them chasing after countless red-herrings and will refuse to see the points he does not want to see.

The man who has trained and disciplined his mind and who is able and willing to use it constructively will think a problem through. He will have the versatility required to examine and assess new evidence. His self-assurance in critical decisions and under pressure of persons and events will be based, not on ignorance or prejudice, but on knowledge. Those who are accustomed to interviewing a great variety of people will know that such people stand out, but they are distinguished not so much by the natural power of their intellect as by its integrity. It is not something with which we are all born, but something which most of us can acquire. Many people begin to achieve a tough mental discipline through university or professional examinations in an exact science, but this alone is not enough; it is necessary to keep the mind at full stretch for several years more before the habit becomes ingrained.

To those who have not faced the problems, stresses, and strains of industrial life, these last paragraphs may seem somewhat discursive and academic. But those who have to make critical decisions affecting the material well-being of their fellows will know the misdirections of human effort that can be caused by sloppy thinking. The commonest failing in industrial management today is not that people will not work the hours or the overtime, but that they will not put their minds to work. This is something which a boss may suspect, but which he may find difficult or impossible to bring home. It is something that may take a long time to catch up with us and may indeed never catch up at all—except with our successors!

It is this quality of intellectual integrity that Christians, above all people, should possess. Our creed is that we are here to serve not ourselves but others; we should, therefore, be much more conscious than others of our standards of service. The standards we set ourselves should be higher and tougher than others set for us. We should look more closely and critically at our performance than they do. We should put ourselves into the shoes of our boss, our colleagues, and our staff and workers. Seen through their eyes, what do we look like? Industry has its fair share of people who are bogus. What they think when they look at themselves in the mirror is their own business. But there is a large gray area in which people are capable of deceiving themselves as to their true worth and performance; at the very least Christians should examine themselves to see that they are setting themselves high standards and keeping to them. Too often the Christian is no better than the next man.

While high standards and an honest mind are essential, we should not belittle the value of sheer hard work. Long hours alone are not enough, but a Christian is called to use his talents to the full, to work with all his might, to run the race of life as if there were only one prize and he must obtain it. A race is not run, it is true, in a flat-out spurt, but it does require determination and endurance, the ability to keep going when others have stopped, and the reserves for the spurt when occasion demands it. All this sounds melodramatic, of course, to the man of the world, a little unnecessary and liable to spoil a man's health and his enjoyment of the natural pleasures of life. But those whose lives and happiness are dependent on the results of our work do not see it that way. The men in the plant and their families depend on us to find the markets to keep them in employment, and to maintain the level of technical expertise and efficiency that will keep their firm competitive. They do not grudge the manager his necessary relaxation, but they know the difference between the manager who is working and one who is cruising. The Christian should be the man who is known in the jargon as "the self-starter." He does not require pushing; he hardly needs supervision. He goes straight for the tough problem and cracks it. When a critical decision has to be made, he is the one who will have done his homework. He may not, of course, be an attractive character in society. We can exaggerate the antipathy of the educated aristocrat to the ideal of hard work, but dedicated as many of them have been to duty and public service, the image of the gentleman as a man of leisure has gained sufficient respectability to be an ideal to many people who ought to know better.

Today there seems to be a feeling that we are reaching the saturation point in personal wealth and that soon we ought to invest not in goods, but in leisure. Whatever others may decide for themselves, this attitude would seem to be wrong for Christians. The excessively long hours of the past were onerous and made it difficult for a man to carry out his responsibilities to his family and his church. But working hours now are not normally unreasonable, and there can be no case for sitting back when there is so much want in the world. Even in Britain and the United States, the care of the aged, medicine, and education are almost bottomless pits, and it will be a long time before their needs are satisfied. Abroad, hundreds of millions are living at no more than subsistence level, and many of these primary-producing countries are dependent on a high and rising level of activity in the industrial nations for any increase in their own low standard of living. "Trade, not aid" is their slogan. In fact they need both aid and trade. In a country like Zambia, a slight drop in the price of copper due to falling demand can wipe out a whole year's revenue in aid funds. However, our duty to work arises from clear and explicit instructions in the Bible and not indirectly through our duty to our neighbor. Many of those who first followed the Protestant ethic had long since satisfied their own small personal needs. In an age when poverty was regarded as an ineradicable evil, they went on working regardless, because the Bible told them that this was right. It is just as well for us that they did.

ROOTS OF THE "PROTESTANT ETHIC"

It is worth pausing for a moment to look at the various traditional attitudes toward work and business that have become woven into British society and have affected American society as well. We are influenced by them in more ways than we might suspect, so that Christians coming from different backgrounds are too often more influenced by those backgrounds than by their common faith. The original "Protestant ethic" is perhaps seen in its purest form in the Scottish attitude toward work and education. The Scots seem to apply themselves to work and self-development with more wholehearted zeal than the English and—though it might be difficult to prove—they seem to be more successful in business and the professions, for their numbers. Until recently a much higher proportion of Scots went to college. The Scottish educational system can be traced to the Reformation and to John Knox in particular.

In England the Reformation was less thorough, and the tradition of the country was not broken as cleanly as in Scotland. South of the border there remained, side by side with the attitudes that arose from the Reformation, attitudes that remained medieval and aristocratic in their lineage. It would clearly be foolish to try to fit all the pattern of English life into two tight straitjackets or to father every attitude today on one of these two traditions. Both had much that was good and much that was bad. But although the older line of thought contained a high sense of personal duty and much else that was good, it contained little or nothing of the duty to work. A gentleman might be called upon to lead, but he was not called upon to work. It was not the aristocracy of England that was responsible for the Scientific and Industrial Revolutions.

This attitude has been modified outwardly under pressure of public opinion, backed by political power that was previously lacking. But it is still apparent in Britain in many unexpected places. A country that sends so few of its best-educated young people into industry and trade, when it depends on these for its very existence, must have compelling reasons. The country whose social leaders invented the Long Weekend may be thought to be less than wholehearted in its attitude toward work. These things should put us on our guard and should perhaps cause some of us to examine, critically and from first principles, the traditions in which we have been educated and the influences which have affected those traditions.

Hard work and education were as much part of the tradition of

Methodism as they were of the Scots Presbyterians, and Methodism had a great influence on working-class men. Professor Postan thought that their application to their work was one of the main forces of the Industrial Revolution and one of the factors, therefore, that enabled Britain to pull itself up by its bootstraps. However, the force of Methodism in Britain has waned and has been replaced by the traditions of organized labor. Not all of these can be traced to Christian sources. Many of them stem from a feeling of genuine grievance at the sufferings of the working class. They saw these as arising from a system that appeared to regard labor as a commodity rather than a calling. Indeed, the church's apparent connivance in this system of society, which seems detrimental to the interests of the individual, may be one of the reasons why the masses are outside the church today.

The dominant traditional attitudes toward work in the United States have been closer to those of the Scots Presbyterians and English Methodists than to those of the English aristocracy. But the emphasis on hard work has waned in the twentieth century, and to the extent that it survives, the motivation for it has in large part changed from a Christian one to an individualistic, materialistic one.

The British tradition that appears to reflect the Protestant ethic most strongly is the code of the professional. In our law, our medicine, our civil service, our armed forces, we British have a tradition of professional competence, public duty, disinterested service, and financial integrity that it is difficult to better anywhere else in the world. Sometimes this professional code is incorporated in the rules of professional institutions, but more often it is a tradition handed down from generation to generation. This tradition engenders the mutual confidence necessary to enable people to trust others with their interests. It is a cement that binds society together, but because it works so well we hardly notice it.

Similar traditions strongly influence the behavior of professionals in the United States also, but professional organizations have not always enforced their codes of ethics adequately. Sometimes the traditions have served to protect members of the professions who are guilty of malpractice, by preventing other members of the profession from testifying regarding the malpractice in open forums. It is only when we go to countries which have no such traditions—and unfortunately there are all too many of them—that we realize the damage to the fabric of society which results from the lack of such standards. It may seem too much to claim such a close correlation between the Christian faith and standards of professional conduct, but it is in the Christian and Protestant countries that these standards are most commonly found; and every Christian who is a professional will agree that his faith and his professional standards go hand in hand.

THE WORK ETHIC IN DECLINE

As the twentieth century draws to a close, the Protestant work ethic is in visible decline. All the talk is of shorter working hours and greater leisure. As the buoyant economic optimism of the fifties and sixties ran out, so workers were more inclined to lower the pace of work in order to keep their jobs. The technology of the industrialized countries is being taken up by countries that have their own kind of ethic. In East Asia the old, disciplined cultures of China, Korea, and Japan have adapted themselves swiftly to take up the new scientific methods of manufacture. No one who has visited Singapore, Hong Kong, Korea, or Japan can fail to be impressed with their technical mastery and skeptical of the idea that the older industrialized countries can now ease up and work half-time. Compared with Eastern cultures, the Protestant culture rests on individual responsibility. A man and a woman answer directly to their Creator for all they do with the talents He has given them. Eastern cultures fit more easily with the collectivism of mass production. Maybe by trying to force society too far into that collectivist mold, we risk breaking the feeling of personal responsibility, which is still a very powerful force in our culture. Certainly collectivism creates impossible dilemmas for Christians as they try to reconcile group-oriented consciences with decision.

The author has had some revealing conversations with a young Japanese businessman, a senior official in one of the big zaibatsu, who became a Christian. He felt an intolerable strain between the big company's demand for absolute loyalty and his own sense of right and wrong. The company kept him apart from his wife and family, a situation that he believed as a Christian to be quite wrong. It demanded from him and his colleagues hours of work that removed any possibility of private life, and it demanded most of Sunday to entertain clients, which prevented him from worshiping as a Christian. It allowed senior and inept officials to rely on this discipline to cover their own weakness, and there was no external moral code against which the aims and methods of the company could be judged. The discipline of the company and of the nation were the automatic responses of age-old tradition. There was no rationale for the tradition, no core of belief, no flexibility in judging particular cases by general principles because there were no principles.

He believed that the system was so brittle that it could not last, because the generation now coming through the universities would not stand for it.

This man may have been reflecting his own newly found Christian disenchantment rather than the real feelings of the new university graduates. Those who deal with the Chinese and Japanese find that their group-oriented system does have some resilience. There is a great deal more consultation at all levels before a decision is made, so the decision-making process is more tedious. But once the decision is taken, there is a much stronger commitment and it is less easy to overturn or undermine. Yet a lifelong dedication to a materialist machine without any other rationale than group loyalty does seem to be a brittle basis for any society. It certainly does not seem to be a course that the countries with a Christian culture would be wise to follow.

Christians are often criticized for being too individualistic, and there is a lot of talk about "structural sin," which appears to refer to the embodiment of human selfishness in the structures of society. This criticism overlooks the Christian's own group, which is the church. We believe in individual salvation, which the church cannot gain for us, and in individual responsibility before God, for which the church cannot substitute. But we also believe in the collective authority and discipline of the church, though this may not be too much in evidence today. Therefore, there is a sense in which the Christian is the real collectivist in a shattered and atomized society. So he feels less than most the need of another group, such as the labor union or the company, to which he can give his loyalty and from which he can claim some identity. And just as the Christian cannot unload his individual responsibility even onto the church, so he certainly cannot unload it onto the union or the company.

The rise of the unions comes originally not from the Protestant ethic but from the employers' lack of it and from the rise of the large, impersonal factory run by an even larger and more impersonal company, which left many workers without job security and without influence over their economic and working conditions. The degree of unionization today corresponds roughly to the size of the factory, and in Britain the time lost in strikes corresponds directly to the numbers employed, rising sharply in establishments of over 1,000 employees and becoming so bad at 5,000 employees that some employers there now believe that size to be unmanageable.

The twentieth-century development of the mass-production line turns the workers into a traction engine, and this is utterly opposed to the Christian's view of the dignity of man made in the image of God the Creator. Its failure in the countries with the Protestant ethic is logical. The answer, as these countries are beginning to discover, is to take it apart and begin again with smaller plants in which small groups of workers can make their own products. The author asked the chief engineer of Volvo whether this would not be impossibly expensive and was told, "There is nothing more expensive than a big production line which is not producing because no one will work on it."

As director-general of Britain's National Economic Development Council, the author once did a study on the economics of scale. The study concluded that although there were strong financial and commercial economics of scale, production economics of scale beyond 500 to 1,000 employers were very hard to find. On the other hand there were very real and substantial production diseconomics of scale. At the time, in the height of the mergermania, strong vested interests resisted this view, but it now seems to be much more generally accepted. Yet lax monopoly laws and strict laws against marketing agreements in both Britain and the United States push companies who want commercial economics of scale into a complete merger, resulting in larger, less manageable, and more impersonal organizations. Tax legislation also encourages small family businesses to sell out to large and less personal public companies and is another trend in the wrong direction.

Meanwhile there is a further danger that the collectivism encouraged by big business and state monopolies will damage the strong work ethic that lives on in professionalism. The dedicated professional must set his own standards, because he is always trying to improve the state of the art, to extend his profession's base of knowledge. Solzhenitsyn's *First Circle* shows how, with all the powers of the totalitarian state, it is impossible to supervise the knowledge worker. No one can force him to find a technical breakthrough, because there is no means, which does not depend on trust, of supervising those who know more than you do. The scientific method is a personal discipline, and anyone who has had responsibility for a scientific budget knows how hard it is for anyone else to judge whether the money is being well spent.

THE PROFESSIONAL DUTY

The professional owes a duty not only to his discipline, but even more to his client. The nurse and doctor owe a duty to the health of the patient, the engineer to the safety of the public, the accountant to public trust in the integrity of those who hold its savings, and the lawyer to public justice. It is these personal obligations that mark off the professional. The professional manager cannot borrow from the bank one day and, by his own actions, risk its security the next day to further his own personal claims in the company. He cannot recruit employees and the next day lock them out on his own account. He cannot give a delivery date today and frustrate it tomorrow.

The professional's institution is his ''collective,'' but professional bodies have traditionally believed, rightly, that it is not their job to act as labor unions. The squeeze put on professional earnings by the twin pincers of inflation and progressive taxation has made many professionals wonder whether this high-minded attitude can continue; this has, in fact, led to some professional organizations—such as those representing schoolteachers and nurses—acting as unions in the United States. But the majority have always concluded that it is better to keep clear and distinct in the public mind the vital contribution that the knowledge, discipline, and service of the professions make to society and to rely on public and political opinion for their continued protection. If the Christian ethic of work is to survive and flourish again, then the bastion of professionalism should not be allowed to fall.

The Christian doctrine of work should lead to the creation of wealth, not by the destruction of the world's natural resources, but by their proper use. Christians believe that mankind holds the natural resources of the world in trust from God and that these should not only be passed on to succeeding generations intact, but, as in the parables of the talents and the pounds, improved in the passing. No generation should leave behind deserts and dustbowls, nor should they leave natural hazards. It requires great skill and ingenuity to improve standards for a rising population, to lift the poor off the poverty line, to feed the starving. It should not be done by squandering natural resources, and the weight of poverty is much too heavy to be lifted by simple redistribution. New ways have to be found of creating and distributing wealth, and this calls for immense dedication and very hard work by those who work in the countries that are the dynamo economics of this world, especially by the professionals who control these economies. It requires political skill too, because the obstacle is not technical knowledge; rather, it is our ability to organize production, to put our immense technical knowledge to work, to encourage investment, to get men and women to work willingly in teams and not to take advantage of their position to take more than they contribute, but instead to put more in than they take out. Our theoretical knowledge is way ahead of our ability to apply it, because its application depends on trust in one another—trust by the investor in the company and mutual trust by those who work in the company.

It is the duty of each generation to re-examine its attitudes by Christian standards, and it is to be hoped that we, in our generation, may rediscover the sense of purpose which a Christian should have in his earthly vocation and the sense of harmony which we should have with the world that God created for our use.

2 The Christian Attitude Toward Wealth

THIS ATTITUDE TOWARD work on the part of a Christian results very often in a substantial increase in wealth. It is noteworthy that the Bible does not condemn wealth in itself. It is not money, but "the love of money," which is the root of all evil. The fruits of the earth are the gift of God and not to be despised. The bounty of nature is here to be used, and there is enough for all if only we have energy enough to lay claim to it. It may be that God uses poverty to bring people to a sense of spiritual reality, and it may be that some, like the apostles, are called to a life of poverty; but poverty brings suffering and great distress, and this cannot be an end in itself. Oxfam and World Vision have brought this home to us in a most direct and compelling way.

The teaching of the Bible would appear to be that it is not the amount of a person's wealth that matters; what matters is the method by which he acquires it, how he uses it and his attitude of mind toward it. Paul tells Timothy, "As for the rich in this world, charge them not to be haughty, nor to set their hopes on uncertain riches, but on God who richly furnishes us with everything to enjoy. They are to do good, to be rich in good deeds, liberal and generous" (1 Tim. 6:17–18). Paul has a positive attitude toward the good things God has given us, because they are from God. He does not try to curb our worldliness by belittling God's provision for us. Instead he teaches that we must share our possessions. Here, as elsewhere in both Old and New Testaments, we are taught to rely not on material possessions, but on God. Nor are we to set our minds on riches. As Paul tells Timothy earlier in the same letter, "There is great gain in godliness with contentment; for we brought nothing into the world, and we cannot take anything out of the world; but if we have food and clothing, with these we shall be content. But those who desire to be rich fall into temptation, into a snare, into many senseless and hurtful desires that plunge men into ruin and destruction. For the love of money is the root of all evils" (6:6–10).

These temptations are common to rich and poor alike. If we are poor, we must not become obsessed by the desire to become rich. If we are rich, we must sit lightly on our riches. James tells us that the rich man must "boast . . . in his humiliation, because like the flower of the grass he shall pass away" (1:10). He must take care that his temporary riches do not make him arrogant, because he and his riches will both shortly perish.

WRONGFUL ACQUISITION

Throughout the Bible there are passages dealing with the wrongful acquisition of wealth. We have, of course, the specific and overriding commandment "You shall not steal." Jeremiah pronounces "Woe to him that builds his house by unrighteousness, and his upper rooms by injustice; who makes his neighbor serve him for nothing, and does not give him his wages" (22:13). James condemns those who use their riches to oppress the poor (2:6) and those who keep back the wages of their laborers (5:4).

We are forbidden to increase our wealth by the oppression of those whose poverty makes them defenseless. The possession of wealth has traditionally given power to its possessors. In agricultural countries, this power is exercised by the concentration of the great estates in the hands of the wealthy families. Where there is no alternative employment, those who are without means have to work on the terms offered by the wealthy. In these conditions, it is clearly wrong to use this power to exact terms that do not give the employee the wages that are available as a result of his labor. I should think it equally wrong to aggregate wealth with the purpose of improving one's economic bargaining position as an employer, or to take steps that would weaken the independence of one's labor force.

There is usually sufficient alternative employment in industrial countries to strengthen the power of most skilled or semi-skilled workers to resist oppression by the rich. But in some cases, members of racial or religious minorities and those with few skills do not have many employment opportunities. In an industrial as opposed to an agricultural community, the alternative of self-employment as a craftsman or a small-holding peasant is not normally available, and where there is oppression it is liable to be much more severe. Any government purporting to act on Christian principles should, therefore, aim to protect the citizen against concentration of economic power and should take positive steps to ensure that the citizen has plenty of alternative sources of employment. Any employer acting on Christian principles should cooperate with such a policy. We might note in passing that a concentration of industrial power in the hands of the state does not of itself guarantee that the state will not use its monopoly position wrongfully.

The object of the Bible's prohibition of usury seems to be similar. In a country of small holdings, a crop failure could be disastrous for the farmer who did not have some ready resources to tide him over. In these circumstances, those who held the resources could hold for ransom those who did not and force them, by rates of interest in excess of the earning power of the property, either to mortgage their property or to sell it. The right thing to do in the circumstances was to help your neighbor over a bad spell and not to take advantage of him. This abuse is quite different from the present practice of charging interest at a rate that can be covered adequately by earnings. But the principle can still be applied today. No one should exploit his neighbor's misfortune. The use of capital to do this is still wrong. Wealth is a trust to be used for our neighbor's good and not his harm.

Perhaps the most odious method of making money is to trade on people's spiritual fears and desires. Money gotten in this way is denounced by both Paul (1 Tim. 3:3; Titus 1:7) and Peter (1 Peter 5:2). The elder who rules well and the teaching elder must not only be paid, but are worthy of "double honor" (1 Tim. 5:17). Nevertheless, church leaders must serve without thought of financial gain. In the present penurious conditions of the Christian churches in Britain this is perhaps not a very pressing temptation, but in other days and in other lands preachers have been known to pitch their message to suit the frame of mind of their wealthier supporters. The difference between this and the selling of indulgences is only a matter of degree.

Most people in business are interested in their personal power in their own company. They want security, freedom of action, and the least number of awkward questions. In the great public corporations, with net assets worth tens and hundreds of millions of dollars, personal wealth is normally too small to be a factor in the balance of power within the company. At the other extreme, the private company is directly controlled by its owners. In between is a growing area where directors hold a minority interest and, by means of these personal holdings, control the company. In the case of a small company with many small, individual holdings outside the board, it is rare for more than 15 percent of the stockholders to reply to a proxy vote, so that unless something appears to be obviously wrong, a board holding of 20 percent is adequate for control. Even in a critical situation, a board holding of 35 percent is normally considered unassailable.

There is obviously something to be said for an executive's having a stake in the business that he is directing. Much good has come from the sense of trust which generations of the same family have had toward the business they have built up. There is little doubt that the worst abuses of capitalist theory have been avoided because the owner of a business could decide that, for the sake of his workforce, he would not exact the maximum profit from his business. Family-controlled businesses are not in danger of involuntary takeover by those who want the maximum return. While the threat of takeover remains and while companies are socially accountable only to a limited extent, the conscientious owner will feel obliged to hold onto his shares for the sake of his employees, and the less conscientious owner will hold on for his own sake. But if there were some social and political accountability—if the owner could be assured that, when he gave up his guardianship, other competent hands would take it up—there is much to be said for the diminishing of unfettered personal control.

Complete personal power over a small business of one hundred people is unlikely to go to anyone's head; but personal power over an empire of 5,000 people is another matter. The eighty-eight-year-old chairman of a $200 million company with thousands of employees was once succeeded as chairman by another member of the family, aged twenty-four. It may be that both were the best possible members of the whole enterprise to be chairman, but one is entitled to doubt it. Executives are in charge of the country's means of production. Insofar as they understand the expensive and complex instruments under their control and use their full potential, the country will prosper and will be able to help and defend less fortunate countries. Insofar as they use their power to neglect the dull or difficult but important jobs in favor of jobs that may be fascinating but are relatively unimportant, or have around them people who are congenial instead of people who are competent, they diminish the wealth otherwise available to the whole community.

Wealth is not always used to buy power. It can also be used for self-indulgence and ostentatious display. It is clearly wrong for the Christian to use it in this way. What is not always so clear is where the line is to be drawn. Increasing wealth brings increasing obligations, and it is only too easy for those who do not have the obligations to criticize the establishment and expenditure of those who do. A recurring theme of the New Testament is that Christians, especially Christian leaders, should be "given to hospitality." This is a quite specific obligation to those Christians who have more than the average share of worldly goods, and life would be the poorer if every Christian limited his establishment and table to cater to himself and his immediate family. Most Christians who have been students or strangers remember with gratitude some Christian household where they were made to feel at home, where they made friends with other Christians or even made their first encounter with Christianity. Christians are not told to be without worldly goods, but they are told to share with those who are less fortunate such worldly goods as they have.

Christians, however, ought to be different in the way they spend their money. Certainly there seems to be no case for Christian expenditure on extravagances that vary from generation to generation under the title of "status symbol." The essence of this type of expenditure seems to be that its price exceeds its intrinsic worth of utility or beauty, because it confers prestige on its owner. A Christian need not live between the gasworks and the linoleum factory if he can afford to live somewhere more salubrious; but he almost certainly should not spend three times as much as he need on a house just because a temporary fashion has created an insatiable demand for reconditioned townhouses in center city. It is not necessary for a Christian woman to be dowdy, but neither is it necessary for her to order all her dresses from Paris. It is right that a Christian should want a good education for his children, but it is almost certainly wrong for him to spend money in having his children educated in purely snobbish values.

While some Christian values remain in society, the Christian will not appear other than abstemious and unextravagant. It is only when society or some classes in society have thrown over Christian values that the Christian who has to live among them may be thought cranky. But it is worth bearing in mind that although Wilberforce and the Clapham Sect may have been thought odd by Regency society, it was the Evangelicals and not Beau Brummell who had the most lasting influence on English social standards for the next half-century. And it was the Evangelicals, including evangelists such as Charles Finney, and not the members of high society who had the greatest influence on American social standards in that period.

There is no logical reason why a Christian should not have a perfectly sober and sensible attitude toward money, but the warnings in the Bible indicate that this is not as easy as it appears. Only one of the succeeding nine commandments is said to be a breach of the first and greatest commandment. In both Ephesians 5 and Colossians 3 we are told that covetousness is idolatry.

Our Lord has told us that the first and greatest commandment is to love the Lord our God with all our heart and mind and soul and strength. If we make an idol of wealth, we put it in God's place and this is a breach of the first commandment. It is therefore a sin we should take particular precautions to avoid. There are two dangerous features to this sin: one is that it is respectable, the other that hardly anyone is ever aware of committing it. A Roman Catholic priest once said that he had heard confessions to every known sin except the sin of covetousness.

RESISTING TEMPTATION

In view of its seriousness and subtlety, it might seem that a wealthy Christian is justified in taking quite specific measures to avoid temptation, by putting beyond the reach of his personal enjoyment such capital and income as are not required to provide an income for himself and his family should he become incapacitated. Some Christians have, in fact, done this. In one case it was done by outright gifts of part of the capital to various causes and the transfer of another part to a charitable trust set up for the purpose of the donor. In cases where the whole capital has been given away without any provision for the family, relatives who are often not Christians have been left to pay the bills for family disasters and even for education of children. This is not a case for going to dramatic extremes, but for quietly drawing a line at a certain point, for putting the temptations of wealth firmly and irrevocably aside.

Most of us, however, are not wealthy or ever likely to be, and our temptations may not be so easily overcome. Poverty does not exempt anyone from the sin of covetousness. It was not to the rich that Paul wrote, "Be content with such things as ye have." The problems of covetousness exist for every Christian. We must agree that there is nothing wrong in material possessions. A comfortable home, a garden, holidays, machines which take the drudgery out of housework, enjoyment of music—all these are good in themselves and are not to be despised. The man who works to give his family these material benefits and to provide for the future does nothing wrong. A man must provide for those of his own household (1 Tim. 5:8) and the parents lay up for the children (2 Cor. 12:14). But we must do so by honest work and not by preferring our claims over those of others, or by exploiting a shortage of our particular skill. A Christian businessman should try to make the maximum profits only where profits are a true indicator of economic service, and he should not maximize profits where to do so would be to exploit his special power over the worker or the customer. A better objective is to maximize economic performance to give the best value to the customer, the stockholder, and the worker. Only if the customer and worker have the sanction required to support their own interests will it be possible that maximization of profits and maximization of economic performance amount to the same thing.

Where a Christian is considering alternative jobs, he clearly should not allow the material reward to be the primary consideration. In some cases he will find that a higher salary is offered to offset the lower standing of the firm making the offer or the uninteresting or insecure nature of the job. On the other hand, between firms of equal standing, salary may be a measure of the worth of the job, and a Christian who sees a higher salary being offered for a job for which he is qualified is not being covetous if he puts in for it. He is right, all else being equal, to go where his services are of most value.

The Christian's overriding rule is that he should sit lightly on worldly wealth. If he disciplines himself to do this, if he avoids setting his heart on any material possession, if he can contemplate the loss of possessions with equanimity and regard their possession as a matter of indifference, then he will be less likely to fall prey to the sin of covetousness. He should increasingly realize the truths that "moth and rust . . . corrupt, and . . . thieves break through and steal," that he came naked into the world and must depart naked out of it. Above all, he should grasp the contrast between this world and the world to come. The saints, who in this world were "tortured . . . stoned . . . sawn in two . . . killed with the sword . . . destitute, afflicted, ill-treated—of whom the world was not worthy" and who wandered in "deserts and mountains, and in dens and caves of the earth," will receive their final reward in the world to come. The man of the world does not believe in this "pie in the sky," any more than the humanist. A Christian should be no less anxious than a humanist to relieve poverty and misery in this world, and in doing so he will follow his Master's example. But if someone professes to be a Christian and does not believe that God will finally perfect His creation, and if he believes that "the dead do not rise," then, Paul tells him, Christ is not raised; "and if Christ has not been raised, your faith is vain." If he believes these truths, a Christian will sit lightly to this world and its passing benefits. His possessions here will be incidental, and he will be more open-handed with them. He will not press his claims on scarce resources to the damage of his neighbor. He will not be guilty of the sin of covetousness, which is idolatry. He will find no insuperable obstacle to giving the church its tithe or more than its tithe.

As the jet and television have made the world smaller, Christians in the industrialized countries have become more conscious of the appalling poverty of the Third World and naturally want to do something about it. Oxfam, World Vision, and other groups have grown to meet this need. There are those, as there have been in every age, who feel that the only answer to the enormous gap between rich and poor is for every Christian to take a vow of poverty and live on subsistence level. Other Christians wonder uneasily whether they are right.

It is especially important that each Christian should examine his own calling. It is only within the terms of that calling that we can decide our right level of expenditure. Missionaries in a very poor country will be especially careful not to put too wide a gulf between themselves and the society where they are called to serve. And there may be those in rich countries who are called to demonstrate by their example that the current standard of expenditure in their own society is selfishly high. But, as Paul has said, each must stand or fall on his own conscience. We are not to judge each other. We do not know the pressures put upon our fellow Christian by his calling. A surgeon, carrying the lives of others in his hands every day, needs living conditions that keep him alert and fit. Many others could live a much simpler life if they had jobs that allowed them the time to grow their own food, build and mend their homes, and walk everywhere they went. But their pay may tell them that they are better employed in creating wealth for others than in an exercise of self-sufficiency for themselves. If everyone in the industrial societies tried to live at the poverty-line self-sufficiency of the poorest countries of the Third World (and some are a lot poorer than others), the dynamo economies of the world would slow down and the Third World would be without hope.

THE THIRD WORLD

Poverty in the Third World needs careful analysis. Although it cannot be denied that colonial powers and other high-income nations have contributed to economic problems of many Third World countries, there are internal causes of poverty in many of these countries as well. The attitude toward work held by many in the Third World is not very organized. The discipline of the industrialized countries is hard to come by in much of the Third World. Even the discipline of regular hours of sleep cannot be taken for granted; the author has found construction sites where the main problem was to keep the workers awake. But perhaps the biggest problem of all is the lack of financial integrity of many in high places. It is not so much that officials levy a toll on every commerical transaction, but that where everything has its price, the whole commercial and industrial life of the country is reduced to uncertainty. No one can ever be sure that the simplest contract will be fulfilled.

An old friend of the author was a senior doctor in a hospital in his own country which was under a military dictatorship. En route to the hospital, all the drugs were replaced with placebos and the drugs were sold for cash in the markets. The rate of inflation was horrendous and price control put all goods, including food and the simplest household goods, under the counter to be sold at black-market prices. All the surgeons and physicians at the hospital were kept on fixed wages, and most felt forced to charge for "free" treatment in order to get enough money to feed their families. My friend, who refused to do this, took his courage in both hands and found an opportunity to tell the military ruler to hand over to an elected government. The dictator's main anxiety was how to be sure if he did hand over that he and his colleagues could keep their corrupt gains, or at least be indemnified for their actions in office. He knew he couldn't rely on promises, and the only way ahead he could see was by hanging on. My friend applied for an exit visa which was immediately granted. The ruler was eventually displaced and shot. This sordid pattern can be repeated in many countries in the Third World. The international business community, far from wanting to exploit them, steers as far clear as it can, both to avoid being involved in the corruption and because they are not geared to the wearisome delays and frustrations.

The author once visited a small but very effective international aid organization. They had no problem raising money for projects. They could, of course, find plenty of worthwhile projects. They had no real difficulty in recruiting and training able nationals to take over projects and run them. Their real frustration was that time and again the new project had to be put in charge of the president's nephew, who had absolutely no idea how to run it. Their own trained leaders were put aside, and the project never fulfilled its aims.

The first necessity for the creation of wealth is honesty. It is the only sound basis for trade. It does no good to those who have to live and suffer under oppressive regimes if we pretend out of misplaced courtesy that corruption is not a major cause of poverty. If we are to help those who need help, we must recognize what stands in the way. Although there is corruption everywhere, regular trade is often less vulnerable to it than official aid, so the increase of trade with the Third World is usually the best way of bringing help. The rise in the demand for commodities means far more to them than any amount of aid, and the drop in demand can never be filled by aid. This is why it is important to keep the dynamo of industrial society running. It is also important to allow a steady increase in imports of manufactures and food from the Third World under agreements like the European Community's Lomé Convention, which is especially aimed at helping the developing countries of Africa, the Caribbean, and the Pacific.

Yet we must not forget our personal contribution. Although neither Old nor New Testament can be said to make the donation of the whole of a Christian's wealth mandatory, there is a strong case for a mandatory tithe of a Christian's gross income. The tithe is not just a command of the Mosaic law; it seems to be a general principle preceding the Mosaic law and succeeding it. Abraham paid tithes of all that he had to Melchizedek. The letter to Hebrews in the New Testament recalls this incident and, quoting the Psalms, points out that Christ is a High Priest after the order of Melchizedek. So, if it was right for Abraham to pay tithes to Melchizedek, it is surely right for us to pay tithes to Christ. If there is any legalism in this command, it can only be the limitation of our giving to the tenth. We are free from the limitation of the law to give more! Christ told us that our righteousness had to exceed that of the Pharisees and Sadducees; He rebuked them for giving only a tenth of the less important parts of their income. Indeed, the tithe may be as good an indication today as it was then of the divide between a nominal Christian and a real one. "Where your treasure is, there will your heart be also." Demands that Christians with heavy responsibilities to hundreds of people live in the simple lifestyle of the bush may be impractical. But the tithe is not impractical and it cannot be laughed off. If we really want to help the Third World, the best way to raise substantial funds in the industrialized world is to teach tithing.

We should tithe our gross income, not our net, for the tax we pay covers the amounts that government pays collectively on our behalf. In any case, the British government allows the church, as it allows other charities, to recover tax. A taxpayer can donate funds to a private charity in such a way that the charity recovers the income tax he paid on the funds if he is prepared to do so for a period that may exceed three years (the four-year covenant). Mechanisms are available that give the donor flexibility in switching his giving among various charities from year to year. American arrangements are even simpler. Americans can deduct contributions to churches and other charities from their income subject to federal government taxation, if they itemize deductions.

The covenanting system not only helps with tax, but improves the discipline of regular giving and transfers the money straight from our own account to the tithe account; so we are never tempted to spend the money that should be set aside, as Paul told the Corinthians. The author has never met a Christian who has regretted tithing. Malachi told the restoration Jews that they should tithe and that God challenges them, "Try me," to see whether He would not reward their faithfulness. Christians today who have put God's bounty to the test will agree that their remaining 90 percent always seems to go further than the 100 percent went before. Faith is believing that if we obey God, He will honor us. He always does.

3 Economics, Politics, and the Christian

MOST CHRISTIANS HAVE become chary of the pronouncement of those churchmen and others who attempt to ally Christian teaching to their own particular political views. It sometimes seems that preachers have become politicians, and politicans preachers. For this reason, many Christians have been reluctant to give time and attention to the relationship of their faith to social problems and have felt that their best contribution was personal piety and the simple proclamation of essential truth.

In the long run, persistence in this view would be a pity. It is necessary for every generation of Christians to make a conscious effort to disentangle the principles for which they stand from encrusted social attitudes and to restate those principles in their relation to new social forces. This is something very different from the attempts to mobilize the churches behind particular political campaigns or parties. The church cannot subscribe to broad political platforms that include many issues on which it is not qualified to comment; but it must be in a position to advise its own members on matters of conduct when they find themselves in unchartered seas, subject to stresses and strains and conflicts of loyalty for which there is no apparent precedent in church teaching. A church that does not attempt to grapple with these new situations is in danger of encouraging its members to lead two different lives, one of traditional Christian morality in the family and the church, and another for weekdays when "business is business"—something the minister cannot hope to pronounce upon or even understand.

No one has put this better than R. H. Tawney:

> No change of system or machinery can avert those causes of social malaise which consist in the egotism, greed, or quarrelsomeness of human nature. What it can do is to create an environment in which those are not the qualities which are encouraged. . . .
>
> During the last two centuries Europe, and particularly

> industrial Europe, has seen the development of a society in which what is called personal religion continues to be taught as the rule of individual conduct, but in which the very conception of religion as the inspiration and standard of social life and cororate effort has been forgotten. . . . Possessing no standards of their own, the churches were at the mercy of those who did possess them. They relieved the wounded and comforted the dying but they dared not enter the battle. . . .
>
> Christians are a sect, and a small sect, in a Pagan Society. But they can be a sincere sect. A good Pagan is not a Christian. The Church will not pretend that he is, or endeavour to make its own Faith acceptable to him by diluting the distinctive ethical attributes of Christianity till they become inoffensive, at the cost of becoming trivial. It need not seek to soften the materialism of principalities and powers with mild doses of piety administered in an apologetic whisper. It will teach as one having authority, and it will have sufficient confidence in its Faith to believe that it requires neither artificial protection nor judicious understatement in order that such truth as there is in it may prevail.[1]

The evangelical emphasis on personal salvation has tended to the view that this is the sole purpose of the church and that apart from personal salvation, little can be done for fallen humanity.

In dealing with the world outside the church, a Christian must balance the doctrine of original sin with the doctrine of common grace. We are told that, despite the presence of evil, God is everywhere present in the world of His creation, upholding all His creatures in both being and activity (see, for instance, Acts 17:25, 28; Col. 1:17; Heb. 1:3). Some divine influence is granted to all men, and mankind is restrained from the worst effects of sin. Only in exceptional cases does God withdraw the restraint completely and "give them over to a reprobate mind," allowing sin to work out its full destructive consequences here.

The church is the instrument of saving grace, but both church and state are instruments of common grace; the responsibility of the Christian in either is not limited to the work of conversion. The church has a duty, not only to preach the gospel, but also to preach the moral law. Individual Christians in a position to influence the standards of society

---

[1]*The Acquisitive Society,* (Harcourt, Brace and World, 1946), ch. 11, pp. 176, 180, 184, 188.

must try to indicate as best they may how the standards of the moral law should affect the issues of the day. This has seldom been as important as it is now, when standards of behavior are lower in Britain than they have been for a long time and when most of the professing church seems intent on having no standards of its own. A Christian should not overestimate the power of common grace. It will not make people regenerate. But neither should he underestimate. "Thy will be done on earth, as it is in heaven" is a prayer we are commanded to make, and it would be lack of faith to wonder whether God has the means to answer it.

Part of our difficulty arises from the different teachings on the relation of church and state. The Erastian view is that the church is dependent on the state; the Roman Catholic view that the state is dependent on the church. The view of the majority of Protestants today is that church and state are essentially different and rightfully independent. Both owe their origin to God, but were instituted for different objectives, the state for promoting and securing the outward order and good of human society, the church to advance its spiritual well-being. Their powers are different. The state has powers of coercion; it "does not bear the sword in vain." The church can use instruction, reproof, censure, and excommunication; but when these means have been used, its powers are exhausted. Finally and perhaps most important for our purpose, the administrations are different. The hierarchy of the church has no authority in matters of state, and the rulers of the state have no authority in the affairs of the church. Where a matter is unmistakably spiritual, the church has a right to speak with authority; where the matter is political, she has no right to speak in her capacity as a church.

THE VOICE OF CITIZENS

This does not mean that the voice of Christians should not be heard in political matters or that they should not influence legislation. What it does mean is that they should enter the arena as citizens and stand or fall on their own merits without calling in aid the authority and reputation of the church. There has been a long tradition in Britain and the United States of statesmen who have professed the Christian faith, have put forward political policies based on what they conceived as being Christian principles, and have appealed for support to the consciences of individual Christians. In Britain the best known are Wilberforce and Shaftesbury, but the line must include many of those who promoted the great Reform Bill of 1832 and runs from Pym, Hampden, and Cromwell to Gladstone and in this century such dissimilar characters as Stafford

Cripps and Lord Hailsham. In the United States the line includes the abolitionists in the nineteenth century and William Jennings Bryan, Woodrow Wilson, the prohibitionists, leaders of the civil rights movement, and the anti-abortionists in the twentieth century. One does not have to agree with all their views or vouch for their doctrinal purity to make the limited point that they acted in this tradition, trying to apply what they conceived to be Christian teaching to political policy wherever they thought it relevant.

When we come to tackle particular issues, we realize that the church is wise to avoid squandering its collective authority by *ex cathedra* pronouncements on this problem and that. Any practical application of Christian principles must take into account a whole host of technical details. There is no point in coming to a conclusion that may be perfect academically but unattainable in practice. It was not enough to be in favor of the general principle of cleaning up corrupt precincts; the ideas had to be clothed in a series of detailed and practical proposals. If universal suffrage was not immediately practicable, then where was the line to be drawn? If the ignorance of the workers argued against it, then how should the workers be educated?

But as soon as we get down to details, a whole series of options opens up. Two groups of equally sound and earnest Christians might—because of slightly different backgrounds, information, and experience—come to quite different conclusions. One might well be right and the other wrong, but the outsider would not necessarily see this. A later generation tackling the same problem would almost certainly modify the original proposals in the light of experience. It is quite wrong for a church that teaches eternal truth to be identified with any particular dogma in the shifting world of political ideas. But it is both right and desirable that groups of Christians should be continuously engaged in the task of working out methods of incorporating the eternal ideals of their faith in practical proposals to meet the changing needs of daily life.

This is the age of the economist. It is the age in which all our debate is centered on the relative merits of different economic systems. Are we for communism or capitalism? Are we Monetarists or Keynesians, for or against wage-price controls? Will socialism give a faster rate of economic growth? Should we be in the European Community? These are the broad points of public discussion and provoke much impassioned argument on all issues, major and minor. Indeed, the medieval disputations on the number of angels that could stand on the head of a pin are nothing compared with the more esoteric arguments of modern economists. Both disputations have in common that certain fundamental information is always missing, and as a result no one can ever prove his point.

ECONOMICS AND CHRISTIAN VALUES

In deciding on the impact of an economic system on Christian values—and it does have an impact—we need to distinguish between the economic system as such and the political system that sanctions or enforces it. The tendency today is to give blanket denunciation or support to the combined political and economic system of a country. It is true that a particular economic system and a particular political system may seem to be interdependent, and sometimes it may be difficult to distinguish them; but if we are to pass moral judgments, we must make this effort.

The different forms of economic organization can be broadly distinguished from each other in the way in which they own their means of production and the way in which they coordinate them. Under pure communist economics, resources are centrally owned and centrally coordinated. Under pure capitalist economics, ownership and coordination are decentralized. In wartime economy or emergency conditions, resources may be centrally controlled while ownership remains decentralized. Under traditional socialist economics, ownership is centralized, but large areas of coordination remain decentralized. Of course, this is an oversimplified picture. All kinds of practical pressures have modified the purity of these economic doctrines. Most socialists do not now believe in the central ownership of all "the means of production, distribution, and exchange." Nor can most communists believe that every single commodity can be centrally planned and distributed without the use of the price mechanism. Capitalists are now moving toward the idea that central planning has its place in the system. Consequently most economies are a mixture of the four basic patterns.

This broad classification does not exhaust the possibilities. Even where there is no centralized public ownership of resources, it is still possible to have centralized private ownership if one company obtains a monopoly; and even where there is no centralized public direction, it is still possible to have centralized private direction by agreement between the companies in the industry. It is also increasingly common to have centralized ownership with a large degree of decentralized direction. Many large conglomerate corporations operate in this way, as do some cooperatives. There is, therefore, a wide variety of methods of economic organization that can be put together in a considerable number of different combinations; and they are not necessarily put in the same combinations by supposedly similar political systems. It may well be that a particular combination under a dictatorial political system is harmful to Christian values, while the same combination under a democracy would be beneficial. A democracy can agree to put the economy under central direction in wartime, and much good may come from the realization of common purposes and interests. But a dictator can use central direction to maintain himself in power and to suppress individual liberties.

What are these values that a Christian should wish to promote and preserve in economic and political life? What are the harmful tendencies against which a Christian should be particularly on his guard? Three doctrines guide him. First, that man was made in the image of God and is individually accountable to God for all his acts. Second, that he is responsible for his fellows; He is to love both God and his neighbor. Third, societies and their leaders are accountable to God for all their deeds.

A Christian, above all people, respects the dignity of the individual. He may be even more conscious than others of the baser sides of human nature. But this brings him to have compassion on his fellows and not to despise them. "There, but for the grace of God, go I." He can still see, through all the degradation, something of the original image of the Creator. He can see the possibilities of transformation, even in this life, to something better and more worthy. He knows the power of God to change the most debased man or woman into a saint. He knows that contempt of his fellows is a sin. He believes that the Son of God was "despised and rejected of men." He understands that he must love even his enemies. To the Christian, no one is outside the pale. No one, however degraded and hostile, can be dismissed as of no account. Onesimus the slave had as much standing before God as Philemon the master. Although the apostles did not directly challenge the existing structure of society, their teaching made it impossible for slavery to continue alongside a devoted, effective Christian church.

This teaching of the dignity and responsibility of the individual cannot be safely divorced from specifically Christian doctrine. When it is so divorced, the "rights of man" tend to become the rights of society, society becomes an end in itself and the individual has been sacrificed to the will of the state. The Christian, like the humanist, may believe that a man is wrong-headed and antisocial; but, unlike some humanists, he should not endeavor to coerce him. If a person has broken the law, a Christian believes he should be given the punishment which justice demands of a responsible individual, because "the powers that be are ordained of God," but would be chary of attempts to treat him as an irresponsible member of society who must be conditioned to the view of the majority. Although a Christian believes his views to be right and believes in his right to express these views, his respect for the individual must extend to those who disagree with him.

CARE FOR OUR NEIGHBOR

The duty of compassion and care for our brother and our neighbor is taught from beginning to end of the Bible. The second commandment is that we should love our neighbor as ourself. This is second only to our duty to love God. In the story of the Good Samaritan, our Lord makes it clear that anyone who crosses our path can be considered our neighbor. Our Lord, when commissioning the disciples, gave them the whole world as their charge. Paul tells the Galatians, "As we have opportunity, let us do good to all men, especially to those who are of the household of faith."

While the Christian is concerned for the freedom and the good of others, he is also very concerned that society should be so organized that people can practice and preach their faith without persecution or coercion. He is much more sensitive than the man of the world to the possibilities of coercion, and he is more aware of the force of intolerance beneath the thin veneer of official tolerance. He is normally better informed on the broad areas in the world today where people are still imprisoned and outlawed for their faith and where the preaching of the Christian gospel is an offense. For all these reasons, a Christian will be reluctant to see too much concentration of power, including economic power. Christians have known the reality of the vision of the apostle John, "No one can buy or sell, unless he has the mark, that is, the name of the beast" (see Rev. 13:17). The price of liberty is eternal vigilance, and in an age when the loss of a union card may spell disaster for a man in one of the most tolerant countries in the world, this vigilance is necessary more than ever.

Before we look at the various broad systems of economic organization past and present, we ought to put down some general standards arising out of Christian doctrine against which they may be judged.

The essential economic freedom is the right of a person to change his job. As long as he can both leave his job and also find another without hardship, he retains a high degree of personal freedom. If his employer wishes to keep him, he is bound to treat him with respect. But as soon as the situation arises in which a man cannot leave without severe penalties, his liberty disappears and he becomes subservient in greater or lesser degree. In countries where the worker is free to form unions and is entitled to the sanction of withdrawing his labor without fear of reprisal, he is protected, to a large extent, against the whims of the employer (though not always against the whims of the union). For this reason, unions are a very real form of protection, and it is interesting to compare the kind of country where unions have a privileged position with those where they do not.

The persons most seriously affected today by the power of the employer are the nonunionized workers, particularly minorities and unskilled workers. Among managers and professionals, those most seriously affected are unqualified and older managers. The qualified manager (certified in engineering or accounting) has a universally accepted credential that enables him to transfer easily to another post. The younger manager, though unqualified, does not find it too difficult in times of full employment to obtain another job. But the manager over forty-five without any qualification except his experience may not be in a position to argue too much with his boss. Even if he finds someone else who wants him, he cannot normally leave without sacrificing a substantial part of his pension, which, because of high taxation, he cannot do without. It is surprising how few people in a large corporation are really independent. Even the president will think twice before he falls out with the chairman of the board. The reason for this is that in the case of most large companies, the stockholders do not exercise any effective control over the board, and there is no countervailing check on the power of the two or three men in control.

DIFFUSION OF POWER

It would seem that Christian principles of economic freedom for the employee are best met by a diffusion of economic power. Unless there are very special reasons for it, a Christian would prefer, from this point of view, not to see either private or state monopoly. In both cases the individual may well find himself in a position where disagreement with authority prevents him from exercising the skills in which he has been trained, because there is only one employer who can use his skill. It is most unlikely that one body of people is possessed with all the wisdom; and it is desirable that other bodies, possessed of the same intimate knowledge of a complex industry, should be following alternative methods and ideas. It is likely that if an industry is confined to one point of view, there will be a large number of people who are in conflict with authority. The Christian may well be among their number, because he is unlikely to take the cynical view, "If that's what they want, that's what they will get." His sense of stewardship of his labor and other resources that belong to God, and his sense of vocation, will give him separate standards, which may make him less complaisant than the average employee. He is therefore more concerned than many others both with the right to resign, if the requirements of his job and his own standards of work are incompatible, and with the availability of alternative sources of employment.

This difficulty is not, of course, confined to Christians, but is encountered by anyone with professional standards of work. It would be nice to be able to say that such conflicts could never arise in a state-owned monopoly, but this would not be true. Certainly the difficulties inherent in a capitalist monopoly do not arise, but the state monopoly has its own particular difficulties in addition to those that arise throughout industry. These difficulties are far from being imaginary, and unfortunately the trend in industry is bringing them into even sharper relief. The big organization is making demands on people's loyalty that it has no right to make. But if capitalism is far from perfect, it does give at least the freedom to change—albeit often at a significant economic cost—whereas when the state is the sole employer, the individual loses a very real freedom.

The Christian might well consider that it is essential to economic freedom that everyone should be left with some money that he could spend as he likes, so that he could have some say in the way he lives and, as a Christian, provide an income for the church. It is undesirable that the church should depend on the state for its income. There are one or two countries where it has done so with no apparent ill effect; but as a matter of principle it would seem wrong for the state to be the paymaster of the church and much more in accord with biblical principles that Christians should support it directly. This means that, other things being equal, Christians would not advocate an economic system where the worker is paid in kind and has no funds left to personal discretion. It does not mean that we should insist on diverting to private charity substantial funds that otherwise would go to tax revenue. In Britain at present, a rather nice balance is achieved in the four-year covenant described in chapter 2. Previous regulations used to provide an effective ceiling on the proportion of income a taxpayer could divert to charity, and this was intended to prevent large portions of the country's income tax from ending up in homes for stray cats and like beneficiaries of private enthusiasms. Although Christians welcome the new and more generous arrangements, it is hoped that this change can be made without opening the way to abuse.

In the United States, the fact that charitable contributions are treated as deductions from taxable income on the federal level gives, as does the British system, more tax relief per dollar contributed to higher-income taxpayers than to lower-income taxpayers, since the marginal tax rates are higher for the former and they are more likely to benefit from itemizing deductions. A change to a system in which all charitable contributions would result in equal proportional reductions in tax liability would give the same degree of tax relief to all donors, and reduce any danger that large portions of tax revenues would be diverted to the particular private charities favored by a relatively small number of wealthy individuals.

In many parts of the world, society even today is so organized that the surplus left to the individual in freely negotiable form is tiny, and he has scarcely any opportunity to establish a pattern of life independently of his employer. There must be a balance between individualism and discipline, and individualism can run riot; but man was created in the image of God and not in the image of beasts. If some people have lost their dignity and individuality and seem to have lost their creative powers, if they run in a herd like animals, that is because they have fallen from their original estate. We must try to organize society so that they can be lifted up again. Uniforms and barracks may be necessary in a fallen society, but they are not part of the Christian's ideal for mankind.

ESSENTIAL CONDITIONS

If we are to preserve the individual's economic freedom in this day and age, he must not only have an income in cash rather than in kind, but must also have free access to essential goods and services. It should be impossible for any sanction to be imposed against him by the cutting off of essential supplies. In many places in Britain, for instance, the only housing available to the working man may be in the gift of the local council. Cases have been known where candidates for union or municipal office who also hold appointments on local councils have had it made clear to their rivals that, if they do not withdraw, their chances of obtaining a council house are remote. Fortunately this sort of thing is rare. But although local government housing does give good housing at low rents, it is not desirable that all housing should be in the gift of the government. It was the cause in 1968 of the civil disobedience in Northern Ireland. For this reason we should insist that the supply of essential goods be carried on through a number of different channels so that there is no possibility of discrimination by the state, by powerful interests, or even by petty officialdom. The best forms of protection are, of course, our democratic system of government and the rule of law. The former makes our rulers answerable for their conduct, and the latter guards against discrimination; but in these days of specialization, when we are so dependent on our fellows in all we do, the possibilities of discrimination are all too many.

If widely held prejudices exist in a certain area, discrimination can persist even in the absence of governmental actions supporting it. Such discrimination has often occurred, for instance, with respect to access to jobs, education, and housing for racial minorities in the United States. In such cases, governmental action against private discrimination may be necessary if all people are to have the opportunity to fulfill their calling as bearers of God's image.

One has a feeling in reading about past persecutions that they faded out largely through inefficiency and administrative difficulties. In Britain's tightly knit and closely organized society, there would be small hope of this. Were there to be some falling off in the standards of official impartiality, a weakening in political standards, or a strong popular feeling against minorities, the latter could very quickly find themselves in a corner. This deterioration is not at all impossible. We owe more than most people will admit to the moral standards of previous generations, largely inspired by Christian teaching. The teaching has been thrown over, and standards of morals and tolerance are visibly deteriorating. We hope that it will go no further, but concentrations of economic power are difficult to pull apart, and it seems just as well that they should not be built.

Most governments today have as their avowed objective the highest possible standard of living for all their people. This would seem a proper objective for the Christian. If we believe that the world was given us by God for our use, and that we were given the intellect to use its resources and the command to work, then poverty would seem to be a curse that it should be our aim to eradicate. Whatever their demerits in other directions, this is the avowed objective of both communism and socialism, and it is to this that they owe their popularity, particularly in the underdeveloped parts of the world. This is not and never has been an objective of feudalism, and insofar as "pure" and "unrestrained" capitalism is a mechanical system without political objectives, the relief of poverty would be an incidental rather than a declared objective.

Since the publication of John Kenneth Galbraith's book *The Affluent Society* in 1958, there has been much misinformed talk about the subject. It seems to be accepted that Galbraith has proved that all Western society has now reached a dangerous degree of affluence and that it should cease to aim at higher prosperity. Those who have taken the trouble to read Galbraith's book will realize, however, that his argument is more local and specialized. He deals almost exclusively with the United States. The overall American standard of living is one of the highest in the world. Galbraith argues that at this point—a point few other countries have reached—the Americans might recognize that the manufacture and promotion of consumer goods had been overdone and that they might have taxes on the sale of nonessential goods, like the British excise duty, to finance better public services such as a public health service and local authority housing.

Of course, living standards in Britain have risen markedly in the last twenty or thirty years, but the high wages now paid to teen-agers and the good housing available to those who have had their name down long enough on the council list mask the poor conditions in which millions in Britain still live. It ill becomes those who feel that their middle-class comforts are a minimum necessity to declare that the working classes now have enough. It is also unreasonable for those whose fathers paid for an expensive education to deride the tastes and mental ability of those who were educated in classes of forty and who had to leave school at sixteen. The economic advance of all classes is relatively recent and, in the competitive world, relatively precarious. It is difficult to feel that we have yet reached the age when an increased national standard of living ceases to be a proper Christian objective, if the increases in output go primarily to those with relatively low incomes.

But economic growth must not and need not damage real resources in the environment. Believing in God the Creator who made man His steward, a Christian must believe in conservation. Believing that the Creator has designed the universe with a balance in nature which has to be respected, a Christian must be an ecologist. A Christian does not believe that the person in the white coat knows best or that science is the ultimate arbiter of morality. On the contrary, science must be subject to the moral order and has no right to play God. The scientific method arose out of respect for nature that was seen by Francis Bacon and his contemporaries as "the book of God's works."

THE USE OF SCIENCE

So a Christian must be opposed to buying short-term economic growth at a cost of depleting the world's resources or of endangering the natural balance. But if science is to be, as Francis Bacon intended, "for the relief of man's estate," then it must be applied within those limits as fully as we know how. The limits do not remove the case for economic growth; they make it even more vital that the knowledge we have is fully applied and that the frontiers of knowledge are extended even further. The limits also make it even more vital that the increases in output are devoted to meeting the real needs that are still unmet in our world, and not squandered on more unnecessary luxuries.

The computer is an excellent example of the use of science to improve wealth within the limits of natural resources and ecological balance. The computer itself does not use much physical energy, and now as computers get smaller and smaller, the silicon chip, the brain of the smallest computers, can be held in the palm of one hand. This economical gadget, the computer, can be used in industrial design to minimize the use of raw materials. It can be used in motors, with the silicon chip, to minimize the use of fuel and to cut down wear and tear. It can be used too in aircraft to plot an optimum fuel-saving course. Computers are used in companies to minimize wasteful holding of stock. They are the center of the brain-scanner and body-scanner that can pinpoint body growths and may be used one day with laser beams to remove malignant growths without cutting open the body.

The computer can now operate with satellites to plot weather patterns and give warning in time to save crops and animals. And the "green revolution" is the use of science to improve crop yields and keep the world's food output in step with its population growth. The resolution of the energy crisis depends on the application of science to provide oil from coal and to harness wind, wave, tidal, and solar power at economical cost.

The obstacle in development today is not the lack of scientific knowledge. The obstacle to benign development is almost always human—the refusal of the American public to believe that there is a fuel crisis; the refusal of peasants to apply new agricultural methods; the drain of national resources into consumption, leaving no money over to invest in new developments; the lack of trust that leads to fears that all new developments will lead to unemployment; and, over so much of the Third World, the sickly cancer of corruption in high places.

Believing as he does in the dignity of the individual, a Christian must also qualify the objective of economic growth by saying that this should be pursued by persuasion and not by force. This qualification is important, because inertia and encrusted habit are the largest single obstacles to economic growth; it is tempting, particularly in underdeveloped countries, to try to sweep them out of the way. In an agricultural country, it may be obvious to the rulers that in a particular instance, farming with small-holdings is inefficient and uneconomical and will never bring the country's production of food up to the level required to give reasonable standards for the industrial worker. At this point it is tempting to put through a forced collectivization to ensure that farms are mechanized and run as economical units. A government that does not respect the dignity of the individual will take this shortcut, justifying the means by the greater good of the majority that will shortly result. This kind of action may well be ineffective and self-defeating, but even if it were effective, it would seem wrong arbitrarily to uproot an individual from a settled way of life. The majority has no right to demand this of the minority.

PRINCIPLES FOR THE MINORITY

Over the years, ways have been worked out of overcoming the obstruction of the minority in ways that respect their existing position, but remove it as an obstacle to progress. The first principle is that if they cannot be persuaded to change their habits to help the majority, they should be given some financial inducement to change. Customers may not like the idea of a self-service store, and the idea of saving scarce national manpower may mean nothing to old Mrs. Johnson in South Bronx; but when Mrs. Johnson finds that she can get more for her money at the self-service, she is made to place a value on her gossip with the store assistants, and eventually she will decide that it is not worth it. The men in No. 2 Bay may not see why they should change their working habits because the young work-study engineer has come up with some bright idea for doubling the output. But when, eventually, an incentive scheme is worked out and No. 1 Bay are taking home $60 a week more, the majority in No. 2 Bay will probably decide to give the scheme a try, and before long the old way of work will seem rather stupid to all of them.

The second principle is that where there has to be expropriation, there must be compensation. At times, undoubtedly, compensation may seem—and indeed be—unduly generous; but the alternative—expropriation without compensation—is both arbitrary and harsh. If the rich are thought to have too much, then they can all be taxed at a uniform rate according to their wealth. This is equitable. What is inequitable is that particular classes of assets, held by rich and poor alike, should be expropriated while other assets escape. It will almost invariably be found that the rich man has scented the danger a long while before, and that the man holding the asset when the time comes is poor and poorly advised.

As an example, consider that when someone acquires property of any kind, he does so under the law of the land as it then stands. He has the right to remain in possession of it until he gives it up voluntarily, and in this reasonable expectation he arranges his way of life. The government may decide that the law as it stood was unjust to the community as a whole, that it hampered economic growth, and that it ought to be changed. Nevertheless, it must respect the consequences of its own previous attitude, and the changes should not be retrospective; property acquired under existing law should not be taken away again. This is the difference between a change of government and a revolution. The revolutionaries repudiate all previous obligations, while a new constitutional government will endorse whatever obligations were properly entered into by its predecessor. A Christian, believing that God's creation is rational and orderly, must favor a rational and orderly form of government, governed by the rule of law and bringing some certainty and order into men's relations with one another.

While a Christian will not want to overturn existing property rights, he will be anxious to see that property is acquired in a fair and rational way, and that there is no aggregation of private wealth that would result in undue concentration of economic power. A system that taxes wealth on its transfer from one man to another is in accordance with this principle, even if by a progressive rate of tax it ensures the reduction of the great aggregations of private wealth.

There are some lesser but important principles for Christians. The so-called welfare state today ensures a standard of care for those unable to earn their own support. This would seem to be a vital Christian objective. The New Testament is full of injunctions to care for the "widow and fatherless." The economic system should provide an efficient safety net, which, as far as possible, protects everyone who might fall into need. The political argument today is not so much about the principle of the welfare state as about its application. Some feel that to protect the minority who are in want there is no need to have free medicine for all, and there is much argument about public housing tenants who have higher incomes than those in private homes who support them through taxes. However, this is a matter of proper and equitable administration rather than a matter of Christian principle. It is perhaps worth mentioning that a Christian cannot feel that his responsibilities are ended when he knows that those in need are financially provided for. A Christian still has responsibilities of noneconomic nature. Old people require company and time and patience, and other needs which cannot be met by writing out checks.

Christians must qualify the desire for greater efficiency by the requirement that those who produce should be treated with dignity and consideration. Laws regulating hours and conditions of work must be regarded as a minimum. A Christian should work for higher standards for the health and protection of the worker and for those small but significant measures that give him standing in his own eyes and in the eyes of the community. There seems to be no reason why the worker in the shop should not have the same standing as the office worker; and improvement in plant welfare should have its place when the surplus is divided between stockholder, state, and worker.

RECONCILING FREEDOM AND DIGNITY

How, then, do these principles fit in with the various economic systems current in the world? It will be clear that the crux of the matter is to reconcile the freedom and dignity that the Christian demands for the individual with his aims for the eradication of poverty. In the West we are inclined to think only of political freedom, but what kind of freedom can be enjoyed by the Indian peasant with an annual income of $100? By his poverty he is imprisoned in his village, in his social system, in his ignorance and, above all, in his inefficient means of production, which prevents even a hope of escape in the future. We should recognize that freedom to vote is not enough if it does not bring freedom from poverty in its train. Which of the major economic systems best reconciles the twin aims of political freedom and freedom from poverty?

Most Christians feel that communism, while it may aim at freedom from poverty, can hope to achieve this aim only at the cost of an intolerable loss of political freedom. So strong is this view that in most

Protestant countries, communism is not even a live political issue. It is true that communism can have local variations and might be modified if voluntarily adopted in a country with long traditions of political freedom; but there is much that appears to be of the essence of communism that a Christian cannot accept. It is avowedly atheistic and totalitarian, it regards material benefits as ends in themselves, and it allows all kinds of injustice to minorities to achieve its ends. Even laying aside these political objections, the communist economic system with its combination of state ownership and central economic control seems bound to weaken the freedom of the individual beyond the point that a Christian would consider tolerable. There are not many strikes east of the Iron Curtain. Events in Poland since 1980 dramatically illustrate the lack of political and economic freedom behind the Iron Curtain, and the extreme difficulty citizens of those countries have in changing that situation. For all these reasons, Christians who are free to choose have avoided the communist path, even though those who live in communist countries should obey their rulers in all matters that are not essential to their faith.

The countries where communism has gained support have been based for the most part on a static, semi-feudal capitalism, which cared for the rich and powerful, but had little regard for the poor. There is all the difference in the world between these economic systems and the "market economies" of Western Europe and North America, held in check by strong central government, which has enacted social welfare and anti-trust laws which reduce the degree of inequality of income and economic opportunity and power. A Christian cannot support a system that does not have as a primary aim a substantial improvement in the lot of the ordinary man.

The economic systems in the Western world today represent various shades of opinion between capitalist "market economies" and socialist "planned economies." The former emphasizes the freedom of the individual, and the latter the social purposes of economic improvement. There is something to be said for the present compromise, and there is much in the extremes in both systems which would, unsoftened by this compromise, be inimical to Christian ideals. At the one extreme, the wholesale nationalization of industry would seem to give far too great a concentration of power; sooner or later, this would detract from the dignity and independence of the individual. At the other extreme, it is fairly clear that the impersonal market mechanism must give way to, and be governed by, overriding social considerations; it should be our servant and not our master. It does seem, however, that we could do better than a compromise between two extreme positions and that it should be possible to evolve a more positive economic system from the principles we have laid down. The next chapter tries to give a rough outline of the kind of system that could both safeguard Christian principles and embody Christian ideals.

4 The Social Responsibility of Big Business

BUSINESS, IN THE sense of the small family business, is nothing new to the church. It is universal and age-old, and its particular temptations are understood and dealt with specifically in the Bible itself. Scripture teaches, for instance, that to give short measure is wrong and to withhold wages is wrong (see Deut. 25:15; Mic. 6:11; Lev. 19:13; Jer. 22:13; James 5:4). The world of small business is not fundamentally different in our day, and although there are problems, it is not the immediate purpose of this chapter to deal with them. The new forces are big business, the active and extensive direction of economic life by strong central governments, and—in certain countries—the power of organized labor.

These new economic forces are more powerful than the world has ever seen, and advances have been made that previously seemed impossible. In every corner of the globe people who have lived just above starvation level have had their expectations raised and demand a better life. Age-old traditions have been put under strain on a universal scale, as the prospect of high industrial wages has taken labor away from feudal estates and family small-holdings. Individual Christians are involved in these changes as pastors, missionaries, teachers, and parents, but above all they are involved when they are part of the economic machine itself. They do not as "organization people" escape from their responsibility as Christians.

In the last chapter we came to the conclusion that neither communism nor feudalism is an economic system that could command support, though the Christian must agree with the objective of raising the living standards of the poor which the communists profess. We also felt that the extreme positions of capitalism and socialism are not compatible with the welfare, dignity, and freedom of the individual, but that the modifications each has imposed on the other has produced a compromise that is more acceptable, if not ideal. We felt that it should be possible, however, to construct a legislative framework for our means of production that embodies Christian ideals more directly. In contrast to capitalism, where the residual benefit goes to the owner, this framework should be explicitly aimed at the increase of the wealth of the community at large. In contrast to state ownership, it should reserve to the state only what is required to be reserved by the strict criterion of public interest, and should aim for the freedom of the individual in choice of job and choice of expenditure. It should not replace the power of big business with the power of bureaucracy, but aim to limit the powers of both to what was functionally necessary for the proper amount and kind of economic growth, and aim to make these necessary powers more specifically responsible to society. Above all, these aims must be realizable in practice and should, therefore, be fulfilled by adapting the existing system rather than uprooting it.

Many feel that the existing modifications of capitalism are sufficient and that there is no need to go further. Capitalism today is hardly recognizable as being in the same species as the laissez-faire capitalism of the nineteenth century. Big business is accountable to its stockholders and lenders under corporate law. It is accountable to its employees under social legislation governing factory conditions, hours of employment, method of payment, right to unionize, and right to strike. It is accountable to its customers under the laws of contract, the laws governing the description and sale of goods and, more recently, by legislation under the restrictive trade practices acts, which in America are very strictly policed and enforced. Its power is limited by acts against monopoly and, in Britain, by high taxation of both corporations and individuals. No one, least of all corporation directors, could be blamed for feeling that "enough is enough."

GAPS IN THE STRUCTURE

It is only when we look more closely that we see the gaps in the present structure, the weakness of the concepts of social responsibility, and the relative ineffectiveness of such legislation as there now is to embody them. Whatever the theoretical power of the stockholder, it is now generally recognized that it is extremely difficult for stockholders to call to account the actions of directors of big business with widespread stock ownership. The board of a large public corporation is, in practice, a self-perpetuating body. Almost all additions are made by nomination of the directors. The majority of public corporations have boards composed largely of executive directors, and their interests as executives and their interests as directors may not always coincide, particularly when it comes to commenting to the owners on their performance as executives. As a result, these enormous centers of economic power, containing most of the nation's productive resources and the practical outlet for its inventiveness, are in the effective control of self-perpetuating bodies. The best public corporations are well aware of the dangers of inbreeding. They recruit to the board strictly on merit and bring in active, able, and independent people from outside. But for every company that does this, there must be half a dozen where power is effectively retained by two or three people whose ideas and objectives can only be challenged by the long-drawn-out pressure of events. This is not the best formula for maximizing profits, let alone for economic growth and a rising standard of living. The answer of capitalism is the "takeover bid," and the threat of this has no doubt done some good; but this is at best a blunt instrument and at worst disruptive if not destructive.

The disappearance of stockholder control is not a plot by established business tycoons. It is the result of a combination of the competitive framework within which business operates and widespread public shareholding. If business is to compete, it must be allowed to keep private a large measure of information on its position and performance, and this information cannot be kept private if it is given to thousands of stockholders whose interests are not limited to that particular corporation. Even if more information is given than at present, this basic contradiction cannot be resolved within the present framework.

What is true for the stockholder is also true for the employee and his representatives. Their information on the costs, competitive position, and potential productivity of the corporation is strictly limited by the degree of secrecy necessary to the competitive system. It is difficult to believe that the settlement of wage negotiations is at the same advanced level as legislation on working conditions. The union leader does not have the information to enable him to point out in detail the methods by which management might recover wage increases by higher productivity. A weak management in noncompetitive conditions will pass the increase on by raising prices. Or else the bargaining degenerates into threat and bluff instead of being, as it should, a constructive negotiation between informed people seeking a reconciliation of their respective interests.

As a by-product of this situation, power on the union side has tended to shift from the responsible union leaders to the activists, especially in Britain, because when it comes to threat and bluff, the activists are usually more successful. It has been argued that the unions need to reform their leadership. No doubt many unions do not pay their leaders enough and do not obtain the caliber of leadership they should, but the question still remains as to what the unions can do with this caliber of leadership when they have it. Unless they have access to more useful information than is publicly available at the moment, it is hard to see how they can bring constructive pressure to bear on management for improving productivity. But efficient and informed union leaders could do much to raise industrial productivity and compel backward management to adopt methods and machinery that would give greater revenue per worker. This should do much to restore the authority of the legitimate union leaders and to cut the unofficial activists down to size.

ADVANTAGES OF COMPETITION

Despite its disadvantages, competitive capitalism has advantages. In classic economic theory it is the method of protecting the customer. Theoretically it should enable the efficient firms to be the pacesetters and to attract customers, brains, and capital away from firms that are less efficient. It should reward the successful innovator and encourage enterprise. It gives freedom to move from one job to another. It tends to minimize the national effects of mistakes in judgment that any single group of men are bound to make. It is small wonder that to so many lovers of freedom the market economy seems both right and efficient and not to be tampered with. But those who have to operate it do not always see it quite so idealistically. It is at its best in small industries with low capital investment and easily comparable products. But in large and highly capitalized industries, it is almost essential to have some form of price discipline, and pricing methods appropriate to the disposal of surplus stocks of toffee-apples are not appropriate to the pricing of electricity or computers. It is also open to purely speculative disturbance.

The official attitude hovers between a belief that competition is a good thing and the knowledge that strict enforcement could, in some cases, have the most destructive results. The American answer lies in massive antitrust legislation. But legislation is a ponderous and inflexible instrument to meet a complex and changing situation, and no other country has moved so far in this direction. There should certainly be legislation against both restrictive trade practices and against monopolies, and British monopoly legislation should be more effective;

but a more precise and more flexible instrument is necessary to look after the public interest.

Left to itself, competition has some less beneficial side effects. Where action is in the public interest, but expensive, it is less than likely that a company fighting for its place in the market will feel free to accept a burden that its competitors do not have to share. Who will fill their plants with low-priced export orders and leave competition free to take a larger share of the home market? Who will take on the burden of training and retraining to have its newly trained people poached by competitors who have not carried the burden? Who can maintain quality when an efficient competitor cuts it? Who will incur costs to reduce pollution when competitors produce at a lower cost by continuing to pollute? Competitive advertising expenditure must be matched, however excessive its scale. Large capital expenditure schemes of competing companies in the same industry tend to hold back and go forward together to protect each company's market share, whereas the public interest would seem to demand that they be coordinated and phased to avoid swings between too little capacity and too much. There seems, therefore, to be an area, too large to be comfortable, in which the market economy does not automatically look after the public interest.

It must also be admitted that, in the market economy, competition does not have the quick and beneficial effects that economic theory would lead us to expect. Efficient companies do not reduce their prices and put the inefficient companies into liquidation. Movement of capital, labor, and competition from inefficient to efficient is sluggish at best. Ingrained habits keep staff, labor, and customers where they are, long after it would pay them to move. But in any case, our physical, and above all our human, investment in great enterprises can hardly allow us to agree that the best solution is to stand by while one or other of them in charge of incrusted and immovable management goes slowly downhill under the pressure of blind market forces toward the final breakup and layoffs. If our competition is to be more than half-hearted, we must feel that those who come under pressure will be made to put things right before it is too late.

These problems have been examined time and again, but very few viable solutions have been put forward. It is easy enough to see what is wrong, and we have had some brilliant analyses, all of which have faltered and fumbled before a solution. This is largely because of the comparative novelty of big business as an institution and lack of understanding of the way in which it works. Most of the analysts have been academic economists or journalists. Few practicing industrialists have had time or inclination to think out solutions. This, combined with our dependence on big business, makes responsible politicians reluctant to do anything that might interfere with its successful working. This situation is changing. Understanding of the complex affairs of industry is increasing together with an awareness that economic growth is a proper objective. The major political parties are becoming less attached to dogma and are looking for a solution that will best combine freedom and economic growth.

The law in both Britain and the United States has already accepted extensive limitations on the rights of private ownership where these go beyond personal needs. While Christian teaching requires respect for personal property, these limitations would be agreeable to Christian teaching on the respect we must have for our neighbors. Limitation on the rights of property is particularly appropriate in the case of major economic units that are large enough individually to affect the life of the community. These should be directed in the public interest as well as in the interests of private owners. It may not always be easy to define the public interest, but this is no reason not to make the attempt.

From time to time as conditions change, it should be as precisely defined as possible, so that action in the public interest is not arbitrary, unpredictable, or unequal between companies in the areas defined as being of public interest. Major corporations should be accountable for their actions and policies. For instance, it might be decided that policies of companies employing more than so many people or worth more than so many million dollars should be accountable for their policies on exports, the amount, timing, and location of investment, layoffs, training, research, wages, and dividends. This would enable the government to understand the operations of those companies controlling the "commanding heights of the economy." They could then define the public interest and isolate the areas in which, without direction, public interest and competitive capitalism might be at variance. This would enable them to give advice, promote joint action in industry, and take such legislative and fiscal measures as were necessary. It could care for the public interest without the dangers of variety, competition, and personal freedom that it would incur if it assumed direct control of industrial life. This combination of freedom and accountability would seem to answer Christian principles best.

EXERCISING SOCIAL RESPONSIBILITY

In the meantime the competitive system sometimes limits the extent to which any one company can do more in the exercise of social responsibility than its competitors, but not all socially desirable policies require money. Others that do require money are not so expensive as to make a company uncompetitive, particularly if its management is just that little bit more conscientious and efficient. Higher morale gives lower staff and labor turnover, and a cooperative attitude oils the wheels in innumerable ways. Managers do not have to wait for the ideal world to begin to exercise social responsibility. Stockholders can and should be interested in more than their dividend and should express their views whenever they have the chance. Their money should be, as we suggest in a later chapter, invested in companies that seem to serve a useful social purpose and exercise a positive social responsibility to customers, workers, and the community. But though there may be direct benefits from the exercise of social responsibility, a Christian must always act on his principles whether in material terms he gains or loses.

Any analysis of corporate accounts will show that the total of wages and salaries is much greater than the amount of the dividend paid to the owners. So the workers' income from the company is usually much greater than that of the owners. If WI is Workers' Income and OI is Owners' Income then perhaps WI = 10 × OI. In some labor-intensive companies WI = 40 × OI. In very capital intensive companies maybe WI = 7 × OI. In all public companies the figure can be worked out. Yet in corporate law, the legal responsibility of the directors is to the owners by whom they are formally appointed and dismissed. If the owners' interests are not looked after, there may be a takeover bid and the directors will find themselves faced with another and more ruthless group of owners. Boards of directors say that the division of industry is artificial and that a prosperous company will benefit both owners and workers. Management maintains that it is their professional duty to look after the interests of workers and customers as well as stockholders. But corporate law reflects neither of these points of view.

For the last decade the European Community has been looking at worker participation on the German, Dutch, and Danish models and wondering whether it should be extended throughout the Community. In 1975–76 a British Committee of Enquiry sat under Lord Bullock to consider how a system of worker directors might be introduced.

In the original German system, there were two company boards.

Two-thirds of the seats on the upper-tier board were filled by owners' representatives and the other third by workers' representatives. Behind the workers' representatives was an elected workers' council. The upper-tier board appointed an executive board who managed the business and had day-to-day relations with the workers' council, and the system seemed to work well. The shareholdings in German companies are much more closely held by financial institutions than in Britain or the United States and these institutions appointed senior officials to the upper-tier board. Each German industry had its own union, and there was no interunion conflict for the seats on the board or the workers' council.

Following Lord Bullock's report, much of the debate in Britain concerning worker representatives on boards of directors has focused on the question of how such worker representatives should be chosen. The unions want them chosen by the unions or joint union councils within each firm, while management wants them chosen by worker councils representing all workers, union and nonunion. Little progress has been made in Britain toward this kind of representation, but there will be increasing pressure to move this way, because the European Parliment is in favor of direct election by all the work force.

In the United States little interest has been expressed by either workers or management in the question of worker representatives on boards of directors of corporations. In the few cases where worker representatives have been added, it has generally been when the company was in serious difficulty and needed concessions or more-than-normal cooperation from employees—for example, Chrysler and Pan Am.

There are some philosophic difficulties about worker directors in the public sector. Can the workers in a local authority claim places on the city council? The elected representatives are none too keen on that idea. Should the porters and catering staff in a hospital have a seat on the hospital authority? Should those in local schools have a seat on the education authority? Should the workers of a union have a say on its executive committee?

Yet despite these and all other difficulties, the idea of the company as a cooperative where workers have rights alongside owners seems worth pursuing. Its reflection of the dignity of the individual as a worker appeals to a Christian, as does the idea of spreading the responsibility to the worker and establishing permanent machinery for cooperation. This latter point especially makes it appeal to governments of all political persuasions who believe that a wholly disproportionate amount of government time and energy is spent in industrial relations. Most governments would welcome any system that minimizes industrial disagreement and removes the artificial and unrealistic struggle between owner and worker. Only parties who believe that the conflict is a symptom of inevitable and desirable class struggle are opposed to the idea of industrial democracy. So, real and formidable though the problems are, a great many Christians will believe that, as far as they can, they must try to solve them and find a better way.

PROJECTS OF JOINT INTEREST

Maybe the best way is for management and unions to start where they are, without legislation, on projects where joint interest is obvious. When the author was chairman of the British Overseas Trade Board, we ran "Export Year" with the strong support of the unions at national and regional levels and the support of the shop floor in 2,500 export companies. The exercise was considered a great success and was continued first by extending "Export Year" to eighteen months and then by a follow-up under the title "Export United." Most companies had a joint management-shop export committee. We also ran about twenty conferences around the country with shop-floor participation. The response in interest and support from the shop floor was very strong, and the public support for this joint exercise was in marked contrast to anything in which the workers were not involved.

Before this, when the author was director general of the National Economic Development Council, the public interest in and support for joint management-union efforts was a multiple of anything that the management side could obtain without worker support. And when management and unions agreed on a policy at the council, it was rare to find government opposed. So there are tremendous social and economic benefits for successful efforts to bridge this unnecessary gulf.

At present, industrial society is split between professionals who have the knowledge, training, and experience to guide an industrial enterprise but do not have the political legitimacy to lead; and elected union leaders who may have legitimacy but lack the technical skill and expertise. True leadership has to have both legitimacy and expertise, and those who can bring the two together will fulfill one of the major political needs of industrial society. Christians in industry should be in the very forefront of this effort.

5 The Social Responsibility of Labor Unions

FROM TIME TO time we read in the papers that a Christian has refused, on conscientious grounds, to join a union and that pressure has been put on his employer to dismiss him. It would be unnatural not to sympathize with a fellow Christian standing alone on a point of principle against the joint might of union and employer. But whatever our emotions, we must each examine for ourselves the principles involved. What is a Christian view of labor unions, of union membership, and of strike action?

The conscientious argument against joining a union is often based on the injunction, "Do not be mismated with unbelievers" (2 Cor. 6:14). The union, it is said, is a body largely composed of non-Christians, and a Christian, therefore, has no right to be associated with it. The logic of this case demands, of course, that we should not be associated with any other non-Christian body, and some exponents of this view also condemn membership in universities and professional bodies, not to mention political parties. A Christian is thus cut off from the mainstream of secular life around him.

It is hard to reconcile this interpretation of "mismating" with the general tone of the New Testament doctrine, especially passages such as Romans 13. It is much more likely that it refers to a more intimate relationship such as marriage; yet even in a marriage where one partner is subsequently converted, Paul says that a spouse is not obliged to leave the unbelieving husband or the unbelieving wife. But even when the argument about being mismated is excluded, there are still some who are uneasy—or at least far from enthusiastic—about union membership, and it is necessary to examine the pros and cons.

Is a labor union in itself an association worthy of a Christian's support and membership? It is perhaps significant that the countries with the strongest Christian tradition have also the strongest labor-union tradition. We hear of few labor disputes east of the Iron Curtain, Poland notwithstanding. The Christian faith teaches us respect for the individual, and if society respects the individual, he must be protected from the possibility of exploitation by those who employ him. He can and should be protected by law, but law is not sufficiently flexible or versatile to meet the kind of situations that arise on the shop floor.

The law can operate only in black-and-white situations. It can be enforceable against the employer only where there is some firm yardstick by which his actions can be measured. Minimum wages, number of persons in a given working area, fencing of dangerous machinery, employment of children—all are measurable and are, therefore, amenable to legislation. But skill differentials, annual wage awards, and general working conditions are relative matters, and the arguments both ways become too complex for legislation. They are issues for negotiation if they are not to become issues of conflict. But the wage-earner is in no position to negotiate as an individual. If he tried, the negotiation would be hopelessly one-sided. His strength must lie in uniting with his fellows so that he negotiates on level terms. Nor is this enough unless he is able to exercise some means of enforcing his point of view, should persuasion fail. It is commonly agreed that the best way of doing this is the collective withdrawal of labor.

PROTECTION OF RIGHTS

The really effective protection is the right of association combined with the right collectively to withdraw labor. In both Britain and the United States, these rights are thought to be sufficiently important to have the protection of the law. It is true that if all employers lived up to Christian ideals, there might well be no need for unions. But in this imperfect world the employer is no better and no worse than the next man. If we are to be realistic, we must certainly agree that labor unions perform a useful and necessary function. No better machinery has been found to protect the individual in our society as it is organized, and potentially at least unions are capable of much constructive work.

To say that unions are necessary is not, of course, to say that every union is perfect or that the conduct of unionists is always wise and unselfish. Employers find that, as a rule, fair dealing with unions makes for a reasonable response; but there are well-known and much publicized exceptions even to this rule. This itself should not deter a Christian either from joining a union or from dealing with one. If a Christian lives up to his own ideals, nothing but good can come from the encounter. Most unions have a democratic constitution, and if members do not bother to vote, this is hardly the fault of the institution. Indeed, much industrial conflict would be avoided if employers and employees made proper use of the union machinery.

If these arguments are accepted, a Christian should have a positive attitude toward labor unions. They should have a Christian's general support. He should not simply accept them grudgingly as a necessary evil. This goes not only for a Christian who is eligible to join a union but for a Christian manager and employer. Comment and criticism on the affairs of the union should be constructive and aimed to help them to look after the interests of their members and should not be aimed at undermining or damaging their position. A Christian must support an orderly society, and he should, therefore, support those bodies that are concerned with resolving people's disputes with each other in an orderly way. In a number of well-known cases, industrial anarchy within a particular company can be traced back to an original refusal by management to deal with responsible unions. This may have been done with the highest of intentions by a paternalistic management sure that it would always do its best for the workers. But as a result, power on the labor side has either been taken over by irresponsible, self-appointed leaders or, without any clear guidance from management, a dozen or more separate unions have been fighting for the workers' allegiance, have established themselves in separate parts of the plant, and the whole bargaining process has become thoroughly disorganized.

One feels compelled to say this because there is still much basic hostility to unions, particularly among those who are somewhat remote from the industrial scene. To quote the Political and Economic Planning pamphlet *Trade Unions in a Changing Society,* "Sickness and accidents, for example, in terms of time lost are nearly a hundredfold more important than strikes yet they receive perhaps less than one per cent of the public attention." The pamphlet's explanation is that some press comment is unbalanced and, at root, hostile to unionism. Attention is almost wholly devoted to the failings of the unions, and little awareness is shown of their present contribution and their future contribution to industrial relations. The result is to increase the defensiveness of the unions' attitudes, to sharpen their sense of apartness, to give ammunition to those elements in the union movement who wish to prolong the class struggle, and to make all unionists instinctively suspicious of the basic motives behind advice offered to them from the outside.

Even allowing for a hostile press, there is a genuine feeling that since World War II, union power has become excessive and has been used to advance the interests of union members at the expense of the rest of the country. Certainly real wages (after deducting the inflationary element) have gone up steadily, and many of those who are not unionized have had no corresponding benefits. Certainly, too, some prominent union leaders have thrown their weight around in public, and none of us likes to see the growth of private positions of power.

Union power is not, in fact, as monolithic as it appears. In the United Kingdom there are about 11 million union members out of 25 million employees; in the United States there are about 22 million union members out of 100 million employees. As manual work has declined in importance, so has the position of the union in certain key industries.

There certainly seems to be no direct relation between those activities that are highly unionized and those activities where wages have gone ahead particularly rapidly.

If the extent of union power is not so wide as sometimes appears, there is no point in denying that unions do have power and do exercise it, and that anyone interested, as the Christian is, in the dignity and liberty of the individual has a right to examine the facts of this power and the way in which it is exercised.

AUTHORITY IN THE UNION

The right to form unions and the right to withhold labor normally go together, because the right to withhold labor is usually the only sanction available to the working man. It is a principle of British and American justice that the courts will not force one man to work for another, and this principle is at one with the Christian principle of respect for the dignity of the individual. But the right to withhold labor is usually effective only if it is exercised collectively. Any breach of collective action by a minority damages the sanction. If some do not accept the authority of their elected leaders, those who do are placed in a very difficult position. Their action may be made ineffective and they have, by loyalty to their leaders, marked themselves as less cooperative than those who did not strike. There is strong pressure on those who are out on strike to return. The negotiating strength of the union, which is based on its ability to command the support of members, is bound to be weakened.

It is sometimes hard for professional people, who negotiate their own terms of work and whose job demands individual judgment and initiative, to see the need for the worker to accept collective discipline. His sympathy naturally tends to be with the independently minded worker who is prepared to stand up to the union leadership. But those who take this line usually picture the union calling the workers out. Today we are far more likely to find that the person who does not accept union discipline is the extremist and that the union official is counseling moderation. Union authority is indivisible. The authority that calls a worker out is the same as the authority that calls him back. If a responsible elected authority is undermined, an irresponsible self-appointed authority is as likely as not to step into the void.

Although the power of the unions is less than is generally credited to them, and is perhaps more spectacular than real, unions do exercise power and have instruments of power that in particular cases certainly seem to be a threat to individual liberty. Of these the most controversial is probably the "closed shop." This is a factory where membership of a particular union is a condition of employment. It must be said at once that many employers are in favor of the closed shop and far prefer to deal with one union which is in an effective position to negotiate than with a series of quite different unions. It avoids demarcation disputes between unions, and it avoids the whole factory being closed down because of a dispute in a particular section. There can also be a closed shop in a limited part of a factory; although this does not have all the benefits of one union answering for one factory, it still has limited benefits for both sides. If a man joins a factory where there is a closed shop as a condition of employment and he accepts this condition, he can hardly complain about it afterward. The difficulty arises where a union has a large percentage of the shop in membership and does not see why the minority should obtain benefits without joining. It then demands a closed shop; and if any employees stand out, the management is faced with the alternative of a costly strike or the dismissal of employees, who may be long-service employees, about something that has nothing to do with their competence in their job.

The unions say that the desire for the closed shop has often arisen as a reaction against the use by the employers of the open shop to break strikes. In other cases, it has arisen from a pride in craft skill. In yet others, it has arisen through disruption by the minority to the damage of the majority. Ernest Bevin, for instance, tried to get a closed shop in London Transport because of the disruption being caused by a small union led by communists. But perhaps the most general reason is the feeling on the part of the union that all who benefit from a collective bargaining agreement should share in the costs of reaching and administering the agreement by paying union dues.

Recognition and the ability to enforce agreements are the twin pillars on which a union stands and without which it cannot function. In looking at the closed shop, the question the union has to ask is, "Is our bargaining strength enough?" In the experience of most unionists, those who did not join were seldom, if ever, acting for the principles of individual liberty. Only the tiny minority of those who had religious scruples were doing anything more than trying to avoid collective obligations. The unions say that since they are voluntary societies, they have to have some sanction over their members if they are going to achieve anything for them. The only real sanction of a voluntary society is expulsion, but if expulsion makes no difference to a worker (or to a member union of the AFL-CIO), then it is no sanction. In an open shop, expulsion makes little difference, but in a closed shop it does. It is, of course, true that the taking away of a union membership in a closed shop situation is a considerable power to give union officials, and it must be exercised fairly. In case of abuse the individual is protected by law, and this is an area in which the law can operate. Many unions in Britain have a "natural justice" rule, but these are no longer necessary since the British courts will imply the rule even if it is not in the constitution.

In the United States a union can require an employer to fire a worker under a closed shop contract only if the worker refuses to pay regular dues or initiation fees, and a worker who objects to union membership on religious grounds is allowed to give an equivalent amount to a charity instead. And even this limited degree of closed shop is against the law in many states.

In Britain, the Trades Union Congress has usually advised its members not to enforce a closed shop unless they feel it to be absolutely necessary. They take the view that it is hardly ever necessary now to enforce a closed shop to obtain recognition. If half a dozen long-service employees refuse to join, it is usually an unnecessary imposition to require their conformity or dismissal. Organization is a means to an end and not an end in itself. On the other hand, if those outside the union endanger the livelihood of their workmates, they are in the same position as the man who runs a machine dangerously, and action has to be taken to protect those who work with him. The union view would be that the employer is perfectly entitled to disagree with their diagnosis and to act accordingly, provided he is prepared to settle the dispute in the normal way. The unions point out that there is a limit to the number of people they would wish to recruit to the unions on this principle and it is not part of their job, they say, to extend their activities to cover those jobs whose occupants are sufficiently distinctive to deal with employers individually and make their own bargain for employment. There is a need to unionize only if the unions do for a man something he cannot do so well for himself. Though there will be times when a union feels that it must have a closed shop, it does not seem to be an inevitable part of labor-union activity.

THE POWER TO STRIKE

The major instrument of union power is the withdrawal of labor. The strike is the union's sanction against the employer. Even if a Christian agrees that this sanction has been found historically necessary, he may still feel some repugnance at the idea of putting the public to inconvenience or hardship in order to enforce his sectional interests. Even if he feels bound in the end to go along with the majority, he may feel that there should be some Christian standard by which he could decide when a strike is justified and when it is not. As soon as you go into it, however, it quickly appears that it is a very difficult matter on which to lay down general principles.

Strike action often arises as much from a lack of confidence in the other side as from immediate and tangible issues. Two different managements could make exactly the same proposals to their respective union opposite numbers. In the one case the union might accept, in the knowledge that the management was traditionally fair and that this was an honest attempt to make the best possible offer. In the other case, the offer might equally correctly be interpreted to be yet one more attempt by management to backtrack on an existing understanding which, if accepted by the union, would undermine months of patient negotiation. They might feel that in these circumstances a strike is their only method of bringing home to management the folly of prevarication.

Some union leaders allow themselves to be guided by the general principle that they will strike only where they are sure of a broad measure of public sympathy for their case. This is not an infallible rule, because the public may be misled or the matter may be so detailed and intimate to the particular plant that the public can not conceivably judge the issues; but it does, at any rate, take into account some independent judgment of the situation. Reference by both sides to an independent tribunal is perhaps the safeguard against unnecessary strikes, provided both sides are prepared to be bound by the tribunal's judgment. Arbitration procedures now cover a very wide range of union activities. It is not infallible—arbitrators are themselves human, and it is thought by some that it has some inherent defects—but it is very much better than open and irreconcilable conflicts. It is natural and right for a Christian to deplore the use of force to settle a disagreement. A Christian regards patience as a virtue, and he should never be exasperated or stampeded into ill-considered action. He should try all other means before allowing a trial of strength and should always do his best to promote ways and means for rational settlement of disputes. That is not to say he should be weak, but he should use his strength wisely. In industrial affairs as in war, wise negotiators try, by convincing the other side of their good intentions, to avoid wasting the resources of both sides in an unnecessary build-up of fighting strength.

It is not unnatural to ask whether, if it is logical to bind employers by company law, there is any good reason why employees and their unions should not be similarly bound. There is, however, a very real difference between legislation limiting people in their dealings with other people's property and legislation governing the individual's personal liberty to work where he pleases and when he pleases. It is part of our belief in the dignity of the individual that the law in Britain and the United States will not enforce "specific performance" of contracts of personal service—that is, it will not issue an order demanding that you actually perform a contract of service, but will only award damages for breach. As part of this principle, the government will not make a strike a criminal offense, although there are exceptions to this principle in the United States—for example, strikes by government workers are illegal in some instances.

Without departing from this principle, it is hard to make a person's right to work or refrain from working amenable to legislation. If it is desirable to have restrictions, there must be some balancing factor, the removal or adjustment of which provides an extralegal sanction. If the government can give something of real benefit to the union then, as a *quid pro quo,* the union could probably hold their members to reasonable restrictions. For instance, there has been the idea that the government should commit itself to a generous rate of economic growth, provided the unions keep pay claims within a certain overall limit. This had certain inherent defects and perhaps was too general and ambitious to be entirely practical. But though this sort of thing cannot be done all at once, if it were done effectively in a particular area and were successful, the union leaders would be enabled to obtain more general acceptance of this kind of bargain. Once this acceptance became widespread, they would then be able to apply pressure at the edges to obtain general acceptance throughout the movement. But before pressure could be applied successfully, most people in the unions would have to believe that the particular proposition was fair.

There are other minor objections to imposing legal obligations on the unions. The unions point out that companies that have to comply with the provisions of the corporation laws have full-time officers. Labor unions at the same level have to rely on part-time officers, many of whom will not have had any training for this kind of job. There would, therefore, be considerable technical difficulties in carrying out detailed obligations imposed by law. Nor are unions anxious to have the kind of legislation on election and voting that would encourage union elections to become like parliamentary elections. In spite of this, the United States has fairly detailed legislation concerning union governance and internal union financial activity, which has proven to be workable. Unions in Britain feel that they are concerned with mundane bread-and-butter affairs which do not and should not encourage high levels of participation in union ballots. This would arise only by bringing in extraneous issues which have nothing to do with the union's true function and which would only cause disruption to their proper job. They regard communism, as such, as an extraneous issue that has nothing to do with the work of the unions, and senior people in the labor-union movement feel that it is, therefore, a mistake for other groups (for instance, a religious group such as Catholics) to try to organize against them. They feel that this is a campaign on the communists' own ground. They do not want to see the day on which the union has 80 percent of the members vote an issue, because that would involve a public campaign and that in turn would almost certainly bring in issues external to union affairs. Therefore, they do not want the kind of legislation that would encourage such high member participation in ballots.

In Australia a very complete labor act was passed in 1952 which set out to reduce what are called "irritation" strikes. It is interesting that there were 1,276 such strikes in 1950, yet two years after the act was passed, the number was 1,490. One understands that this trend has continued and that the act has failed to fulfill the hopes for it. One is told that if the workers think they have a grievance and believe their only way to express it is by means of a strike, they carry on in defiance of all authority. In the United States, the Taft-Hartley Act was passed in 1947 and is aimed at limiting several union practices that are considered unfair. But although there are fewer strikes per 100,000 employees in the United States than in Britain, the American strikes last longer on average. Workdays lost per 100 employees were higher in America than in Britain in the sixties, but higher in Britain in the seventies. There is, therefore, no hard evidence yet that more legal control of unions would lessen the chance of industrial conflict.

Many people feel that one particular reform which would avoid control by minorities and ensure internal accountability is the requirement that all union decisions, particularly elections, should be by secret ballot. The unions say that they have no inherent objection to the use of secret ballots and, in the United States, elections for union offices by law must be by secret ballot. Although there have been cases of union elections being overturned by the government because of fraud, most union elections are conducted honestly. But requirements for membership ballots on all issues before a union come under the same general objection as referenda in parliamentary government. The best way may well be to give the officers of the union sufficient powers to make the decisions themselves without reference back. One of the reasons for suggesting ballots is their use as a means of controlling unofficial strikes. But the unions feel that the most practical way to do this is to delegate sufficient power from the unions to the local officers, and there seems to be something in this point.

SEEKING A BETTER LIFE

Union ideology is very different from middle-class professional ideology. When someone joins a union, he gives up his individual position in order to gain the protection and benefit of a collective position. He is not interested in competition at the expense of his mates. The essence of unionism is that you do not compete, you combine. Nor is he interested in the threat of international competition. He is inclined to the view that if you really want to be competitive, all you have to do is to live on rice. The union leaders say that manual workers do not just want more money. The aim of a union is to achieve for them something broader, and that is a better life. This might mean the opportunity to develop their personality outside the strict confines of a prosaic job. This could be achieved by shortening the working week or by an extension of the paid holiday.

This is quite different from the professional's aim to develop himself through his work. A professional aims to a far greater extent to assimilate his work into his life. This may seem to many to be much more in accord with the Christian's view of work as a calling. It would seem to the Christian much better for unions and management to try to upgrade the work force from semi-skilled to skilled work, as it has been upgraded from unskilled to semi-skilled, and to give people more responsibility and a bigger personal stake in their jobs. It would seem desirable to make the work itself more dignified and worthwhile.

But the union view would seem to be that the present balance between skilled and unskilled was what they had to deal with and will have to deal with in the foreseeable future. A massive shift from routine work would be a visionary and somewhat unreal objective at present. Nor do unions say that people find routine work degrading. It enables them to occupy their minds with other things. What makes their work tolerable is its predictable rhythm, and it only becomes intolerable if this is upset by hectic or spasmodic pressure. It is very difficult to bridge this gulf in attitude toward work and perhaps too easy for a professional to feel that his view is *the* Christian view. Nevertheless, although it may seem wrong to take an extreme view and regard our work as drudgery—merely something to be got through with a minimum of trouble while our mind is elsewhere—there must be many Christians who cannot foresee a time when they will not have a dull job and who find an outlet in their interests in the home, the community, and Christian service.

The unions are not perfect, and there is much that they could do to reform themselves, both to do their job more effectively and, especially in Britain, to police their own activities at shop-floor level. An industrialist hesitates to tell the other side its job—and the idea that there are never two sides nor any conflicting interests is nothing but a confusing myth—but it seems to be generally acknowledged in Britain that most union constitutions could be adapted to give greater flexibility in meeting new patterns of industry and employment and, in particular, in bringing local shop-floor bargaining back under union control; that they should find a way to raise their dues so that they can pay their officers a more reasonable salary and attract and train able officers for the future; and that they should find means of settling interunion disputes so that these do not cause hardship to those not involved. These are all domestic matters well within their province, and for a Christian who feels the call to this kind of work there would seem to be wide opportunity.

INITIATIVE FROM MANAGEMENT

But the first task of those in management is to make constructive suggestions about their own actions and attitudes. If managers also aim to be leaders, one cannot help feeling that the initiative in good labor relations should be with them. There is a good deal of truth in the old saying, "There are no bad soldiers, only bad officers." In a broadcast talk, published in *The Listener,* W. E. J. (now Lord) McCarthy, Research Fellow in Industrial Relations at Nuffield College, Oxford, says, "Some [mine] pits are more strike-prone than others; some docks are peaceful; certain motor-car firms hardly ever have a strike. If one is to provide more than a very general and superficial explanation of strikes, one has to go beyond industrial generalities and ask why it is that at firm A, or in workshop B, problems solved elsewhere result in strikes." He investigated two coal mines near each other, with similar conditions but very different strike records. One of his main conclusions was that in one pit management was trusted and in the other it was not. This is most people's experience. Anyone who has ever taken over responsibility for a number of factories will know what a difference there can be in their labor relations, and often the cause can be traced back quite clearly to good or bad management.

The union officer does not look for softness in bargaining. What he does look for is honesty and to be treated on an equal footing and not with contempt or indifference. If management cannot concede a point, it is better to say so rather than try to conceal it. The unions' advice to management would be, "Don't be tricky, and don't be brutal." In the words of the apostle Peter, "Honor all men."

As far as the professional bodies are concerned, it has been traditional in Britain and the United States that, although they look after the interests of their members and in some cases negotiate salary levels with the government, they should never improve their bargaining power by a threat to strike. This has partly been because most professionls were not employed in large numbers by a single employer, and the occasion did not arise. It was also partly because a profession embodies an ideal of disinterested public service, and it was hard to see how this sense of public duty could be reconciled with a threat to deprive the public of their professional skill. It is nevertheless true that unless professional earnings are tied in some way to the earnings of those who feel free to bargain, the professions—particularly any whose salaries are fixed by the government—will be at an increasing disadvantage.

Because of specialized skill, the professional is in an exceptionally strong position, and his instinct against using his whole bargaining strength is undoubtedly right. But if the community is so weak-willed that it concedes an improved share in its wealth only to those who threaten it, then the professional may need to reconsider his position. He owes a duty to the future to see that the right quality of person continues to be attracted into the profession in the right numbers; if the differential for six years or more of hard training is not enough to do this, the public will suffer in the long run.

At a junior level some professionals have joined unions, and in Britain the medical profession, which is faced there with a monopoly employer, the temptation to strike has been strong. In the United States some of the traditionally lower-paid professionals, such as teachers and nurses, have resorted to strikes in order to raise their incomes. But the professional who ignores his duty of care removes his special position in society and becomes no more use than a high-paid technician. Many Christian churches advise Christian doctors and nurses not to strike, declaring that they should allow themselves to be defrauded rather than abandon or even lower their duty of care for their patients. The pressures of inflation have put the professions under unprecedented pressure, and society would be extremely foolish to put them to the wall. But professionals do have an alternative. They can organize themselves, not in labor unions, but as professionals; in each of the four major countries of the European Community there are at least a million, and many more if the civil service and armed forces are included. They can offer to negotiate with government that in return for a professional undertaking not to strike, government will ensure that they do not lose whatever premium they need to attract new entrants and maintain the high standards of care that the public needs. This kind of bargain could also be struck, on slightly different terms, with police, firemen, and others who provide public services and on whose devotion to duty the whole of society depends.

6 Power Struggles and Inflation

In the 1960s, economists began to be aware of the operation of an economic factor, "cost-push inflation," which seemed to be at least partly due to rising money wages even when the demand for labor was slack. The response by some was to call for incomes policies in which the labor unions would restrain wage demands in return for government's undertaking to increase the national rate of economic growth.

Bankers and traditional economists opposed the idea, pointing to figures that showed a close relationship between increase in wage rates and the pressure of demand for labor. This correlation, known as the "Philips curve," led bankers and traditional economists to advocate financial restraints as the cure for all inflation. But most countries were not willing to use stagnation and unemployment as the main weapons against an inflation rate that was less than 5 percent a year, and they tried to operate wage-restraint instead. So in Britain there was a National Board for Prices and Incomes. In the United States there were "wage-price guidelines," and in Germany there was "concerted action" between the highly organized employers and the limited number of industry-wide unions.

But in 1968 cost-push inflation increased dramatically. Following student riots and industrial unrest in France, the giant Renault car company made a double-digit wage award to get its workers back to the production line; the British Secretary of State for Employment christened the new factor "shop-floor power." In 1969 the Treasury kept strict curbs on the expansion of the British economy, but the rate of increase in money wages began to take off—greatly to the surprise of the traditional economists and the labor-union leaders. In the United States, restrictive budgetary and monetary policies in the early 1970s raised unemployment, but seemed to have little effect on inflation or wage increases. The economists' "Philips curve" came dramatically apart and now showed, despite a steeply rising cost of labor, lower demand and rising unemployment.

"Shop-floor power"—that is, the power of the production workers—is an economic phenomenon that should hold no mysteries for those who have access to a corporation's accounts and understand marginal costing. But economists do not have access to corporate accounts, and so microeconomics are not well understood, and those in the company who do know and understand are most unwilling to advertise calculations that show their company's vulnerability. Shop-floor power can be represented by a simple equation: If C equals the cost of a stoppage, and A equals the wage award which will prevent the stoppage, then in a large, modern industrial plant, it may be that C = 20A, so it pays the company to settle. In the case of an auto assembly line, it is probable that C = 30A, so it was entirely logical for the Renault company to get their workers back as fast as they could. Since the equation is the same for all the major competitors in an industry and all are under similar pressure from the shop floor, it is easy to pass the cost of the award on in higher prices, and so "cost-push inflation" enters the economy.

THE COST OF A WORK STOPPAGE

There are two main reasons for the sharply increased cost of an industrial stoppage. First, the cost of production labor is declining in relation to the cost of installed machinery and to the less flexible costs of research, administration, selling, and distribution. All these other costs and the depreciation and financial costs of plant continue despite a stoppage.

Second, if the stoppage produces a loss of sales in a competitive market, the cost of recovering those sales can be very high. If the customer is lost permanently, the cost of recovering the sales elsewhere can be crippling. For both these reasons, 95 percent of the manufacturing industry in Britain keeps the show on the road and never shuts down. In the United States, executives of manufacturing companies seem to be more willing to accept long strikes under some circumstances, however.

On the other side, the cost of the strike to the worker in Britain is offset to some extent by the social security income available to his family, and the repayment of taxes reduces the immediate cash loss for a short stoppage. But most potent of all, as the inflationary spiral rises, there is the high cost to the worker of failure to exercise his shop-floor power when others are exercising theirs. Most exercise of shop-floor power is defensive—a panic at being left behind as the wage-price spiral rises. This new power is the same in every industrialized country and has had the most profoundly destabilizing effect throughout the world. And not only do production workers take part in this spiral. Salaries of white-collar workers, including executives, are also usually raised, and prices of products are often raised more than enough to cover increased labor costs, in order to provide for increases in money earnings for owners of the company. The rates of inflation this has produced have wrecked the international monetary system on which the exceptional growth of postwar trade depended; and in the seventies, the rate of growth in world trade slowed right down and unemployment increased to record postwar levels.

The most dramatic destabilization came through the sharp rise in world oil prices in 1973 and 1974. Throughout the fifties and especially during the sixties, the industrialized countries passed on their higher prices to the primary producing countries. The price of finished industrial products rose far faster than the price of the raw materials—including oil—used to produce them, and the gap between rich and poor countries widened. Then in 1973 one group, the oil producers, struck back using an old-fashioned cartel agreement to raise the price of oil to recover what they had lost. This in turn produced strong pressure within industrial countries to recover the lost value of purchasing power; wage rates soared in the industrialized world until by 1979 the relative cost of industrial goods to oil had risen toward its previous level. Then in 1979 and 1980 the oil cartel struck again, and the price of oil soared once more. But the inflation caused by this battle and attempts to fight the inflation with tight fiscal and monetary policies had meantime resulted in 6 million unemployed in the European Community and almost 10 million unemployed in the U.S., with little prospect of any early significant improvement.

Since the exercise of shop-floor power and similar attempts by others to raise their money incomes is more often caused by fear than greed, a government-policed incomes policy can remove the fear that those who hold back will be overtaken by those who go ahead and exercise their power. Incomes policy has also had strong support in Britain from the very large number of employees—probably two-thirds—who do not have the power to bring a huge, expensive industrial machine to a standstill. The teacher's only sanction is to send the children home, and that doesn't cost a million pounds a day. The shop assistant, the clerk, the civil servant, the employee in the small business, the self-employed, the agricultural worker, or the postman cannot pull out the plugs from an industrial empire. The professional worker has a professional duty of care, and a strike destroys his whole professional status. The British incomes policy of 1975 was introduced on behalf of the low-paid worker, whom it was aimed to protect.

To a Christian, any selfish exercise of economic power, any extortion at the expense of the weak, is a sin equivalent to the sin of usury. A Christian believes in wages which are, in the words of the apostle Paul, "just and equal," rather than wages arrived at under the amoral forces of the market—and a Christian certainly cannot believe in freedom to add leverage to market prices by threats of intolerable economic damage. So it might be expected that Christians would welcome a fair wage policy. But incomes policies practiced so far have come in for a good deal of criticism and not all of it has been foolish.

SEEKING A JUST WAGE

There is natural skepticism of the feasibility of a policy that attempts to regulate the detailed wages and salaries of 25 million or more people. The just wage may be a firm objective, but who can judge it? Yet the vast majority of wages are not judged by the job market as people change their work; they are judged at periodic reviews for all employees—not just new employees—by various standards of what is fair. In Britain, each industry and each section of the public service has its negotiating councils and wages boards; similar institutions exist in the U.S., although much wage setting here is less centralized. Within that sector, which may employ a half-million to a million people, there is an elaborate framework for deciding comparability between one grade and another, with formulae carefully worked out for rewarding merit. To ignore these hallowed traditions is to ask for trouble.

What is missing in this periodic process is machinery for connecting these great bargaining circles at the national level. National bargaining is a process of keeping up with the Joneses and if possible trying to get a bit ahead. In theory each worker is bargaining with his employer. In practice each bargaining circle is competing with the rest, for if the employer does not have the resources to pay an inflationary claim, he has to pass it on to customers or else reduce the real incomes of other employees or the stockholders. The only worthwhile national incomes policy is one that can decide what is just and equal between the great bargaining circles. There is machinery for everything else, but not for that. Because no incomes policy so far has ever attempted it, it is an awesomely difficult task, but it is not impossible.

However, incomes policies have a bad name for other reasons. They usually come into operation with a temporary freeze. This quiets the panic, and the desperate scramble to keep up with spiraling inflation dies down. But in the absence of machinery strong enough to settle differentials between the bargaining circles, crude first-stage incomes policy will tend to squeeze the differential of the skilled and professional workers; when they see the reward for their skill begin to slip away, they become very restive. If an incomes policy is to succeed in the long run, it has to respect the need for differentials. If it is biased for one group and against another, it will not have the broad base of support it needs. Any redistribution of incomes should take place through legislation put before the elected representatives of the people and not as an accidental side effect of an incomes policy that has never been argued out and agreed in Parliament or Congress.

A third problem with incomes policies is that they really do need to judge correctly the position and power of the labor unions. Shop-floor power may undermine the power of management, but first and foremost in Britain it undermines the power of the elected officials of the unions. If shop-floor pressures can bring immediate surrender by management, there is no need to send for the union officials, no need to ask their permission to strike. If there is a strike, the union has to decide whether to make it official or to try to exercise sanctions. And what sanctions can they exercise? If they withdraw membership, another union is likely to pick up the members. In the United States, where unofficial or "wildcat" strikes are rarer than in Britain, the membership challenge to elected officials more often involves the rejection by ballot of a contract recommended by the union officials and a call to strike for higher benefits, or the defeat of incumbent union officials in favor of more militant opponents when they stand for reelection. So it is no answer to shop-floor power to curb the powers of the union. The problem is not that the unions have too much power; it is that in controlling the power of their members they have too little. No union leader is ever going to admit to this in public, but they all admit to it in private.

What each union leader has to decide is whether an incomes policy will help his members or not. It is sometimes a finely balanced decision, but logic usually points in the direction of an incomes policy. It is not in the interests of the labor-union movement to have mounting inflation. Their fragile structure is not equipped to deal with the panic that sets in. They do not have the staff to deal with two or three wage rounds a year or to keep control of the union when inflation is out of hand. They know as well as anyone else that inflation destroys the industrial investment on which the real growth of incomes and maintaining full employment depend, that it discourages exports and encourages foreign imports, and that both these trends cost jobs. So the minds of a majority of union leaders are usually open to discuss an incomes policy.

But the labor-union leader must in turn convince his own members not to exercise the full bargaining strength on their shop floor. He finds it impossible to do this if the whole union movement seems to be under attack; he has to persuade members that they are not putting their heads into a noose and that government is acting for their benefit and not against them. And he has to persuade members that restraint in increases will lead to restraint in prices. He has to persuade skilled members that they will not lose their differentials and unskilled workers that they will not be worse off. He has to show some reasonably new prospect that the restraint will pay off. None of this is impossible, but it does require both goodwill between government and the labor-union movement and also skilled negotiation to bring into line the union leaders who feel that previous incomes policies have left their members worse off and the ambitious or maverick leader who wants his agreement to be dearly bought. Finally it needs a supervisory body in which government, management, and union leaders have a continuing say and which none of them can easily repudiate.

There are those who believe that in these negotiations the people's elected government has to concede altogether too much to the union hierarchy and who point to past concessions by government that have greatly increased union power and privilege. They believe that shop-floor power has been strengthened by the inflationary pressure of demand, especially in the early seventies, and they point to countries that have much lower rates of inflation without national incomes policies but with a much stricter monetary policy. And they are supported by a great many people whose real spendable income dropped very sharply during periods of inflation, progressive taxation, and egalitarian incomes policy. So the labor-union movement too has to create a spirit of trust in its intentions. It must not use the pressure on government to "do something" about mounting inflation and unemployment simply as a bargaining lever for its own members.

DIMINISHING THE SHOP-FLOOR POWER

In the long run, shop-floor power will decline as it has risen. Companies in Britain are now well aware of the special vulnerability of the very large plant to stoppage by a few people at any point on a long production line. The optimum size for new plants there is now 500 employees, rising to 800 if absolutely necessary. To avoid the usual damage from stoppages, companies are setting up two or three plants for the same operation, and most companies are buying each of their semi-manufactured parts from several different suppliers. Big companies are diversifying their businesses to give them added financial strength and the ability to withstand strikes. Companies are holding higher stocks of components and finished stocks so that they can wait out a strike. Multinationals can produce the same component in a number of different countries. In Britain the picketing of plants not involved in a dispute has accelerated the trend toward active countermeasures. At the national level, trade associations are considering tougher measures, such as lockouts, to raise the cost of unofficial strikes to the unions.

Government too is inclined to be tougher and less responsive to rising unemployment. There is no doubt, as a mathematical exercise, that if governments refuse to finance excessive wage claims, they will put a lot of people out of work—though not always those who have had the excessive wage award. Hyperinflation in Germany in the twenties was caused by a government that thought that financing inflation was the lesser of two evils. They were almost certainly wrong, and Germany's rulers today believe they were wrong and take a tough anti-inflationary line. But Germany's rulers today find this easier than other governments, for they have to deal with a few large unions, each covering a whole industry, each with seats on the supervisory boards of all the major companies; and they have political support, for the national memory still recalls Germany's hyperinflation. Most important of all, Germany with its strict wage restraint has had the largest and steadiest rise in real income in recorded history.

The question elsewhere is whether a hard-line monetary policy can ever be enough on its own. Is it not necessary for a more acceptable alternative to be on offer, so that as unemployment mounts, government can point to the better way which they would prefer and which is there if people wish to take it? At some totally unacceptable level of unemployment and inflation, people will so wish.

Inflation is a moral issue. Inflation caused by the exercise of shop-floor power or other economic power transfers wealth from those who do not have the power to those who do, from the weak to the strong. It often squeezes the financial resources of companies and reduces their power to make new investment that incorporates new technology and creates new jobs. It reduces savings and diverts them from wealth-producing industry into personal expenditure and puts savings into tangible assets that do not produce wealth: second houses, paintings, antiques, and vintage cars. Inflation reduces government's powers of action and makes it more difficult for the elected representatives to reduce unemployment and improve the nation's resources. It is a cancer that cripples the economy, that grows on itself and prevents normal functioning of the body politic. And the longer it goes on, the more difficult it is to cure, because people adjust to what they experience and it is harder and harder to adjust back to single-digit or to zero inflation.

Unemployment is also a moral issue. Paying high unemployment benefits makes sure that no one will starve and maintains some tolerable minimum standard for those who receive it (although this minimum standard is lower in many parts of the U.S. than it is in Britain). But it is not the same as having a job. People want to be wanted, to feel that they are useful and necessary, that they are making a real contribution to society. The young especially, who have been trained and taught for twelve years at school, who are full of ideas and ideals, want to make a real contribution when they are graduated. It is a double blow to discourage the graduate in particular, but the traditional method of reducing employment in hard times by "wastage"—which means no new recruitment—falls especially hard on the graduate. If we are not prepared to give the young something useful to do for society, there is the danger that they may find something to do themselves in a society in which they have no stake—and that activity may not be so useful.

Unemployment hits some parts of the country far harder than others. In some parts of Northern Ireland, unemployment is as high as 20 percent, and in particular districts it is double that. Not suprisingly there is a ready recruiting ground among the young for paramilitary organizations. Such high concentrations of unemployment are also found in some areas of the Northeastern and Midwestern U.S. In mixed racial areas, unemployment hits some races harder than others. Small wonder that the young of these races seem to be in trouble more often. If society could hold out some hope, give them some vision, they would have a goal toward which to look. When inflation has removed the power of governments to maintain full employment, they can no longer promise a worthwhile future to the young. If society is to give the young hope, it has to find a way to overcome the mistrust and selfishness that keep the young out of useful work.

DIFFERENCES FROM THE PAST

Industrial society is quite different from all previous societies. Employment depends on the industrial machine. Only about 3 percent of British and American employment is on the land, and even that is highly mechanized. In industrialized Germany between the wars, almost 50 percent of the population was on the land. The raging inflation and the heavy slump hit only half of the economy with full force; the subsistence economy of the land underpinned the other half. Today the industrial economies are much more highly geared, much more dependent on smooth and continuous operation, much more seriously disrupted by a slump. And only government has the power to regulate the economy. Even the largest company's sales are only 1 percent of the national product. So however much we may want to decentralize and rely on the initiative and energy of the entrepreneurs, only government can create the conditions in which this initiative and energy can flourish and can provide jobs for the citizen.

But the maverick quality of shop-floor power jams all government's instruments for controlling the economy. Unless the rate of inflation can be controlled, very little else can be controlled, so government is paralyzed. It is certainly unable to plan the economy as socialists would wish. Nor can it hope to create conditions in which savers and entrepreneurs will risk their own money and in which enterprise will flourish and create employment as conservatives would wish. So governments are held in check until they can find a way to control the new kind of inflation without increasing unemployment. No doubt there is some rate of unemployment at which shop-floor power would be held in check, but no one knows what it is and no one knows whether government's nerve would crack before it was reached. It is instructive to note that only recently—when unemployment in Britain rose above 10 percent (adjusted to the U.S. definition) in 1981, and in the United States above 9 percent in 1982—shop-floor power seemed to have diminished considerably. The central issue in the economies of all industrial societies is how to reduce inflation and unemployment simultaneously. That is why, despite all its problems, British governments of both major parties have tried incomes policies three times.

These attempts have left their scars. The biggest scar in Britain is the confrontation in 1973–74 between the Conservative government and the National Union of Mineworkers, leading to the three-day working week for the whole of British industry. Of course, an incomes policy does need to be able to stand up to this. It needs the commitment of the unions, which that government did not have, and it needs the flexibility to give an exceptional award in the knowledge that it will not become a precedent. No government wants another such confrontation, and no government will want an incomes policy without union commitment to agree on an annual guideline and strongly supported machinery for deciding the differentials between the great bargaining circles. The two British miners' strikes had other causes. The big private-sector companies are most vulnerable and concede most to shop-floor power, and there is a tendency for the public sector—which in Britain includes the miners—faced with the whole weight of government anti-inflation policy, to feel that it has been left behind and to become militant. Militancy is no sign of power. The most militant can be those who feel most deprived, and the least militant those who are satisfied because they can get what they want without a struggle. The crowd in view of TV cameras outside the factory gate are often less significant to the result than the quiet accountants behind closed doors, working out that C = 20A.

But, just as the oil sheiks discovered that they had a countervailing power which could reverse the trend that had gone against the primary producing countries, so the miners found in their first strike that they had a power which could offset the trend that had gone against them. They too could stop the production lines.

Secondly, they had a particular grievance. They had been telling the country for years not to rely on cheap imported oil, not to abandon coal-fired power stations. But their industry had been steadily run down because, in the short run, oil was cheaper. Abandoning mines, resulting in huge permanent layoffs of miners, had built up an intense resentment that gave the miners the hardness which any group needs if it is to damage its fellow workers.

However, it was the slippage in their differentials in relation to other workers that triggered the two strikes—a slippage felt by many others in the public sector who, while the private sector goes ahead, face governments that can enforce wage guidelines in the public sector. The strongest practical argument for incomes policy is that the public sector has to have one in any case, and this resentment builds up against the private sector, leading to extensive public-sector strikes. Certainly the majority of large-scale strikes in Britain are in the public sector; and since they challenge directly the authority and credibility of government, they can be prolonged and bitter. Inquiries in Britain into a particular nationalized industry that have no authority to cover the whole of public-sector relativity usually end up with a major award to that particular industry, and this only passes the trouble elsewhere.

THE POWER OF ENFORCEMENT

These attempts have left their scars in both Britain and the United States. In both countries there have been major strikes by workers not content to agree to contracts within the guidelines of the income policies, and in both countries some settlements have been made that did not fall within the guidelines, thus weakening the power of the government to enforce them elsewhere.

But large companies and large plants do exist, the country does depend on them for exports and for jobs and they are unlikely to be replaced at the heart of any of the major industrial economics for ten or twenty years. They are vulnerable, and this vulnerability which exposes the whole economy must somehow be dealt with. Were they all to be nationalized, government would perhaps be in a stronger position to deal with this wage claim—at the price of more monopoly and more concentration of government power; but those who want less bureaucracy would not want that solution.

If the alternative for a decade is a rough-and-ready incomes policy or growing inflation and unemployment, which is the lesser evil? Is there any other way of dealing with the power of large unions and large corporations that leads to less bureaucracy, less legislation, and less industrial strife? No one so far has come up with a better idea than an agreed, union-backed, government-backed, and fair wage policy. In the end a policy that is so widespread in application and so crucial to national economic policy can only be carried out with widespread public support and understanding. The author spent seven years as a member of the National Economic Development Council in Britain, five as its director general, and has in that capacity and others been at the heart of the public debate on union policies. There is no doubt left in his mind that the public regards the level of incomes as a moral issue, that there is a real belief that incomes should be "just," reflecting effort and responsibility, and "equal" for similar work. Incomes are discussed in moral terms and not in terms of supply and demand. The average citizen regards inflation as "wicked" and stable prices as "right." So there is remarkable support for the Pauline ideal of wages that are "just and equal" and for an attempt to find a fair wage policy. There is also almost universal opposition to excessive bargaining power and little love for those who have obtained high wages through its use. Incomes policies lose support when they are seen to be too rigid—squeezing traditional differentials—or too negative, simply used to hold back wages without any obvious corresponding benefit in lower unemployment or higher real incomes.

This debate, which is central to the success of the industrial economies and all the economies in the Third World that depend on them, will no doubt continue over the next decade. It is to be hoped that the Christian ideal of wages which are "just and equal" will make a helpful contribution to the debate and to some longer-term solution. Christians especially will want to discourage those who think they can do better by means of industrial warfare and will want to encourage those who are trying to draw up terms of industrial peace.

7 The Authority of Government

DURING THE LAST century, the role of government in business has grown substantially. Industry has grown in size, rising incomes have raised economic expectations, and governments—particularly democratic governments—have had to pay increasing attention to economic affairs. Anyone in industry and commerce today will become involved sooner or later in government regulation, consultation, and exhortation, not to mention taxation. What is to be our attitude as Christians to government activity? Should we welcome it, oppose it, or just wish it would go away?

There is a strong tradition in industry that deplores government interference of any kind, on both practical and moral grounds. Many Christians find the whole apparatus of politics and government distasteful, at best worldly and at worst, in its use of the law and force, a denial of the Sermon on the Mount. Added to this, there is a restless spirit in the world today. Its heroes are the resistance leaders and revolutionaries. From non-cooperation to fiddling with tax shelters we are "agin the government." However strong these feelings may be, they are not in accordance with Christian teaching.

Government and the family are the only secular institutions that have been ordained by God. Paul says in Romans 13, "Let every person be subject to the governing authorities. For there is no authority except from God." Our Lord told us to "render therefore to Caesar the things that are Caesar's." But He also added, "Render to God the things that are God's." Where there is a conflict between these two commands, the Christian must clearly obey God. But direct conflict seldom, if ever, comes in countries whose laws have been permeated by Christian principles; even in other countries most people, most of the time, are content to be subject to the authority of the Powers That Be.

Those who feel that our ideal in political activity should be the commandment of our Lord in the Sermon on the Mount, "Do not resist evil,'' misunderstand the counsel. This is directed, not to the nations of the world, but to the Christian—and even then, not to the Christian in his capacity as a citizen, but in his personal relations. The world is, as we stated in the introduction, under the law of God, and its lawlessness must be controlled and its vice kept within bounds. God's means of doing this is the institution of government; a Christian, in giving obedience to government, is giving obedience to God's chosen instrument. This is made quite clear in the passage from Romans 13 quoted above, and in 1 Peter 2: ''Be subject for the Lord's sake to every human institution, whether it be to the emperor as supreme, or to governors sent by him to punish those who do wrong and to praise those who do right.''

These passages do not accord with the view that a Christian should not resist evil in any form, and any interpretation of the Sermon on the Mount that does not take them into account must be suspect. It is clear that Paul regarded it as his right to claim the authority of Roman law to avoid wrongful imprisonment at Philippi and to enable him to appeal to the emperor. But Paul, who resisted evil intended against him by those outside the church, made it clear to the Corinthian Christians that they should put up with harm from those within the church rather than submit their claims to non-Christian judges.

In Romans 12:19 Paul tells us that Christians should not take vengeance, and then in Romans 13:4 he says that the one in power is ''the servant of God to execute his wrath on the wrongdoer'' and we are told to obey the power and, by implication, to help him in his task. Therefore, a Christian in his capacity as citizen may have to do something quite out of keeping with the conduct of a Christian in his personal relationships. At least he is to pay taxes so that the police force will do it for him (13:7).

THE QUESTION OF TYRANNY

Other Christians can see some point in being subject to a democratically elected government, but cannot see that it is right to be subject to a tyranny. This is a particularly important point for those who have relations with foreign governments, which are certainly not all democratic. Are we, they ask, to say that the Huguenots who fought for their liberty in France, or the Dutch Protestants who gained their liberty from the Spaniards under William the Silent, were all in error, not to mention the Scots under John Knox, the British Parliamentarians who rose against Charles I, and the Whigs who forced James II's abdication? Or the American revolutionists who fought for independence from Great Britain? Had all those people been forced to the point where they would have had to disobey God if they obeyed the government? Were they not also contending, quote properly, for civil liberties? These are fair questions.

A Christian must, of course, disobey commands that conflict with specific Christian teaching. The three Jewish princes were right in refusing to bow down to the idol set up by Nebuchadnezzar. Daniel was right to continue to pray to his God, despite the laws of the Medes and Persians to the contrary. In our time it is inconceivable that a Christian could have been right to obey the state in killing six million Jews who had not offended against its laws. We are commanded to obey because the power is "God's servant for your good" and "to execute his wrath on the wrongdoer." If the power is a servant of evil, it has to that extent lost its authority. But this necessary limitation does not detract from the authority of government in mundane affairs, and certainly not in the industrial affairs with which we are primarily concerned.

In these days, when rebellion against authority is commonplace and seems, from the dislike of discipline and constraint, to gain general approval, we need to be particularly careful in justifying rebellion and revolution. The religious revolutions of the seventeenth century, however right they may have been, disturbed the general acceptance of the authority of government. They may even to this extent have paved the way for the much more thorough-going revolutions which had nothing to do with religious liberty and which have played some part in the general revolutionary mood of so much of the world today.

When we look at the religious revolutions in detail, we become aware that the leaders realized that they had to justify themselves in regard to the Christian doctrines of civil obedience. In the case of the Huguenots, William the Silent, the Parliamentarians, and the Protestant states in the Thirty Years War, there was—as well as a very real fear for religious liberty—some legitimate questions as to the identity of the Powers That Be. In France the Huguenots argued that the powers claimed by the king were an innovation (*Vindiciae contra tyrannus,* 1579). The Low Countries claimed that they were entitled to obey "the stadholder" rather than the emperor. Even so, such was the respect for law and authority that William the Silent long maintained the fiction of loyalty to the emperor. In Britain, John Hampden argued that the king was not entitled to impose a particular tax without consent of Parliament. The king alone was not the Powers That Be. Even so, the Parliamentarians long maintained the fiction of loyalty to Charles. In Germany it was held that the power resided in the states and not in the emperor. These Protestant heroes cannot, therefore, without serious qualification be cited as examples of the right of minorities to disobey government.

In these days of nation-states and written constitutions, sovereignty is much more clearly defined. Cases where it would be right for a Christian to rebel or resort to force on grounds of disputed sovereignty would seem to be limited. There is certainly no case for taking direct action against a government on the sole ground that it is not democratic. The Roman Empire, under whose rule our Lord and Paul and Peter laid down the general rule of civil obedience, was far from democratic. Christians may prefer democracy and need not pretend otherwise, but in mundane matters they are bound by the laws of the land.

The Christian in industry, when inclined to disagree with his own or another government, must realize that—however wrong-headed or arbitrary government action may seem—he is bound to obey it and support it. This is important, not only in relation to increasing involvement by the government in industry, but in relation to trade in newly independent countries whose governments need support if they are to do their job.

RULES FOR OPPOSING WRONG

In an imperfect world there will be many cases where a Christian—as a Christian—is out of sympathy with the actions of a government or even with the whole system of government. Even if he is bound (as he is) by the laws of the land, he may well feel that it is his duty, within these limits, to oppose whatever he considers wrong. But whatever the wrong, there are certain rules he should follow. First, in his own country, he must act as a citizen. Just as we argued in an earlier chapter that he should not use the influence and authority of the church, so, on a lesser plane, he should not use any economic power he may have as an industrialist. The purpose of a company is to trade and not to rule. The same goes for labor unions, which should not use their power for political ends.

Second, his opposition to the policies of the government of a country in which he is not a citizen should be strictly limited to whatever concerns his business there, and it should be conducted within the legal and social framework of opposition in that country. Third, where there is room for differing opinions, he should take advice from responsible people who are qualified to give it before he launches out. The many newly independent countries are especially sensitive to alien economic dominance and see it as a very real threat to their independence. A Christian may be more tempted than most to interfere, if only because he has high ideals and a sense of responsibility; but however right he may be, he must respect and obey the government of the land in letter and in spirit, and he can only do harm to his faith if he does not.

Earlier we dealt with the general relationship of the government to industry and commerce, the case for and against both nationalization and the market economy. Most of our relationship with the government is on a much more humdrum level than this. A majority of Christians might well agree with the earlier argument against an undue concentration of direct control in the hands of any authority, state or otherwise. But the line must be drawn somewhere. There are areas where an incorrupt and efficient state or local authority can render a better service than competing private interests. There are places where its powers are absolutely essential, not only to provide services that should be communal, but also to enforce standards of health and hygiene and of law and order. Everyone knows the exasperation that can be caused by petty officialdom and the absurdities of long-outdated local laws, and it is sometimes taken for granted that there was once an era of freedom when a man's life was his own, when he did very well indeed without the fussing bureaucrat. If anyone were forced to be precise, he might say that he thought that the rot set in during World War I. Perhaps this attitude is now more common in the United States than in Britain, but there is still a lot of feeling in Britain that any government interference in industrial affairs is, almost of necessity, bad.

In any case, the idea of a golden age of complete laissez-faire is almost certainly a myth. According to George Kitson-Clark in *The Making of Victorian England,* the British government started to try to bring industry under some sort of regulation well before the Industrial Revolution had gained full force. He regards 1833 as the turning point, when an act was passed "which contained provision for the appointment of a board of inspectors with executive powers to put it into effect and to report on the way in which the Act worked." The reports were the beginning of the specialized knowledge of government experts, and the discretionary power was the beginning of delegated powers given to ministers "to be in fact exercised by civil servants."

"Though the tremendous power which was being developed by the Industrial Revolution could and did work for the good of humanity, there could be no security that that was what it would do unless it was brought under conscious discipline, and that discipline could only be imposed by the assumption by the public of constantly increasing discretionary powers to be exercised under the direction of experts, who would draw upon growing experience which only work in that particular department of government could give,'' Kitson-Clark writes. The day of the specialized and powerful civil service department had begun.

The creation of an infrastructure of health and sanitation was necessary to avoid disaster, ''but without conscious direction, privately directed industrial development was most unlikely to do any of these things. . . . Power and knowledge to discipline and to direct and utilize these forces [of the Industrial Revolution] was needed if life was to be lived in tolerable conditions, let alone to improve in quality. That power could only be developed and directed to the right ends by the public authority.'' So the next time the planning authorities are being particularly maddening about some point—vital to us and apparently academic to them—we perhaps ought to reflect that they have been there, and rightly so, since the beginning of industrialization, and nothing is likely to be gained by wishing them away. We can only try to see that they fulfill their proper role better; and this may not mean any loosening of their control or slackening of their inquisitiveness.

If these points on the role of nineteenth-century government appear to be somewhat labored, it is only because there is a natural tendency among Christians to regard views held in a God-fearing, church-going age as a norm, and any departure from them as being necessarily for the worse. It is just as well, therefore, to remind ourselves that one of the promoters of the 1833 Act and much of the subsequent legislation was that great Christian and Evangelical Lord Shaftesbury.

THE PACIFIST ISSUE

It is especially the rights of a government in waging war that have caused most controversy between Christians, and this is a very practical concern of most Christians in industry. With defense spending taking a very large proportion of the national budget, there is hardly an industry that is not concerned with armaments in one way or another. Some industries are almost wholly devoted to it. This is not the place to tackle the pacifist issue at length. Many fine Christians have been pacifists, and their point is clear-cut: ''You shall not kill'' is for them an absolute obligation without any complicated qualifications. One must respect them for this position, and in Britain and the United States, as in other democratic countries, they are respected. But others feel that if the Sermon on the Mount does not preclude maintaining law and order nationally, it cannot preclude it internationally. In both cases law has to be backed by the sanction of force. There can, of course, be wars of aggression on an international scale, just as there can be tyranny on a national scale; but this does not affect the principle.

A Christian's anxiety, as a citizen, will be to find a way out of international conflict other than through war. A country governed by Christian ideals would not be jingoistic, would not throw its weight around lightheartedly, and would not allow itself to be swept into conflict on a wave of fear or hate. But should it, in a world far from innocent, deprive itself of all power of resistance to its enemies? Should it not rather use its power to promote peace? The Pax Romana and Pax Britannica were not unworthy contributions to humanity.

The new dimension in war today is the weapon of mass destruction. That nuclear weapons do introduce a new dimension to war can hardly be in doubt. Whereas civilians have been killed in previous wars, it was, in theory (even if mass bombing had made the theory latterly a little remote from practice), possible to direct weapons almost exclusively at military targets. With the use of atomic weapons this is no longer possible. One must, again, respect the views of those who are not pacifists and are therefore prepared to make and use conventional military weapons, but who would sooner be defeated than make or use weapons of indiscriminate mass destruction, whether atomic, gas, or germ.

It would be wrong for any individual in this novel and most difficult question to say that his sense of Christian values was the only right one, though it is a question on which, since it vitally affects all of us, it is particularly hard to be tolerant. This discussion has gone on over the years and there is little point in prolonging it here. There does seem to be a case both ways, and it would be wrong automatically to condemn a Christian because he was engaged, directly or indirectly, in the manufacture of atomic weapons or the means of their delivery. His hope, as a Christian, would almost certainly be that in manufacturing them he was making more certain that they would never be used by either side. The fact is that many Christians engage in such work with a good conscience. We may disagree with their judgment, but we should not impute wrong motives.

Whether we like it or not, those of us in industry are a part of the whole national effort, including defense. There are strong grounds in

Christian teaching for holding that a country is entitled to defend itself. Although there are many Christian pacifists, most Christians believe that the teaching in Romans 13 and 1 Peter 2 forces them to help the government in a number of tasks that are distasteful but necessary to maintain order in the world. If we accept this, we ought not to begrudge our cooperation, but should participate actively and on principle. This does not exclude our exercising our rights as citizens to make constructive criticism of foreign and defense policies. We should see that the power of arms is used to promote peace and to minimize conflict.

There is an increasing tendency today for the government to bring pressure on industry without putting it under direct legal obligation. Sometimes these pressures and exhortations (for instance, to export) involve some measure of personal sacrifice or inconvenience with the aim of benefiting the community as a whole. In such cases the Christian's duty is clearly to act in his neighbor's interest.

At other times, the government may decide to bring pressure to bear on industry to devote scarce resources to one purpose rather than another. Though, in general, Christian doctrine weighs the scale in favor of authority, if the government's choice appears to be misguided or misinformed, those in industry are not bound absolutely. The very fact that it is a matter for exhortation and not for legislation may reflect some uncertainty on the part of the government on the details of application in particular cases and may also, therefore, reflect a willingness to leave the application in the end to individual judgment.

It is not always possible to act on exhortation if competitors refuse to do so. There is no point in voluntary limitation of dividends if takeover bidders are free to buy the shares at a depressed price and put up the dividend as soon as they have gained control. But it is at the very least required by the Christian's respect for the Powers That Be that he tries to discover the reason for the exhortation and behaves as sympathetically with its spirit as he can.

HELP FOR INDUSTRIES

However strong the feeling against government interference in industry, it does not seem to stop the flow of requests to the government to do something to help particular industries. Nor is there anything wrong with this in principle. An industry ought to be the first to know when foreign rivals have gained an edge on it and when its employees' jobs are in danger. This may be because of the industry's own inefficiency, but it may just as well have to do with the international tariff structures or protectionism by other governments. Even in less dramatic circumstances, it is right and proper that if there is conflict between different groups of citizens, there should be representation to government so that it can act as judge between them. What is necessary, however, is that those who put forward sectional interests should do so in accordance with the best standards of advocacy. All special interests should be declared. Information should not be misleading or put forward in a misleading way. But having declared our interests, we are entitled to put forward whatever arguments we consider should be taken into account, even though our interests would benefit should the decision go in our favor.

For instance, a group of shopkeepers are doing nothing wrong if they band together in an attempt to preserve amenities necessary to the continued use of their street as a shopping center, even if this means the diversion elsewhere of heavy truck traffic and an improvement in their property values. On a larger scale, an industrial district is entitled to represent to the government the consequence of the closing of one of its major plants, even if their remedy involves diverting government contracts from plants in other districts.

Advocacy is not, however, the same thing as pressure, and the essence of a pressure group is, presumably, pressure. Is it right to bring pressure on an elected government? Is this not an avoidance of the agreed method of government? This very much depends on the method of pressure. If this is exercised through the open method of public debate, or even through a statement that unless action is taken the matter will be made public, then this is not, in a democracy, avoiding the democratic process, but a proper use of it. It is perfectly proper to point out to an individual member of parliament or to a government the possible electoral consequences of their actions. Pressure of vested interests is normally thought of, however, as something more sinister and powerful. What people rightly resent and regard as wrong is an attempt to go behind the issue in question and exercise some power over the government that has nothing to do with the real issue and cannot be countered by the other side. Universal franchise limits the powers available to vested interests, but both labor unions and big business can exercise some pressure by refusal to cooperate in areas where government badly needs active help and support. This is as wrong as to threaten direct action to sabotage the action of government.

In an industrial society, industry and government are interdependent. Government relies on industry for investment, exports, employment, innovation, and improved productivity. Companies and those employed by them pay a large part of the country's taxes. If they do well, the government's tax take is high; if they do badly, the tax take is low and government has to pay out unemployment and social security benefits. Industry is even more dependent on government. Export sales and the competition from foreign imports depend on the trade agreements a government makes with foreign countries. Exports and imports both depend on the rate of exchange for the country's currency. The rate of capital investment depends on the prime interest rate, and both exchange rates and interest rates depend on a government's financial policy.

It is government that has to decide the balance between private-sector and public-sector expenditure. And when an economic crisis occurs, it is only government that has the authority and the central national machinery to try to deal with it. Good government can carry a country through the worst crisis. But bad government can wreck even an economy that has plenty of natural and human resources. There are countries such as Argentina with immense natural resources, vast expanses of fertile land, and exportable supplies of food, with hydroelectric power, self-sufficiency in oil, and an educated population, who nevertheless have an inflation rate of 150 percent, no economic growth, and widespread poverty. There are countries like Switzerland—overpopulated, with few natural resources—who yet have scarcely any inflation, excellent public services, no pollution, no unemployment, and one of the highest incomes per capita in the world.

To do any good, government needs the consent, not only of the people, but also of the vested interests, including those who own the industrial machines and also those who operate them and can stop them. It may be that the vested interests are too powerful, and maybe steps need to be taken gradually to make sure that the legitimate government has the power it needs to govern. But a wise government will consult, listen, and try to give reasons when it cannot do what the interests want.

THE ULTIMATE AUTHORITY

But those in industry have to recognize that government is the country's ultimate authority, and if it is blocked by vested interests, there is no other authority. We live in a rebellious age when it is fashionable to be against the government. If in a stalemate everyone could go back to their own garden patch and keep body and soul together, government's lack of authority might not matter. But in industrial society, where everyone is dependent on everyone else, the failure to recognize the ultimate authority of government could eventually be catastrophic. It is easy for a group to prove that society cannot do without them, but almost any other group can prove the same. And all that these demonstrations prove is that industrial society needs a government to arbitrate and citizens who regard that arbitration as final. The teaching of the apostle Paul (Romans 13) and the apostle Peter (1 Peter 2) is that the governing powers are ordained by God and that in secular matters we must obey them even if we do not agree with them.

Governments today are trying desperately to combine full employment with a stable currency. No one else can ensure full employment. No one else can ensure a stable currency.

Our new high-income industrial society needs a stable currency to ensure the economic balance and the investment necessary to achieve full employment. So those who block a government because they cannot get exactly what they want for those they represent, take on themselves a heavy responsibility for the consequent damage. And governments who give way only to those who threaten them and ignore those who respect their difficulties also have a lot to answer for. Governments should not be pushed around, and they should not allow themselves to be pushed around. They should encourage dialogue, as the British government does in the National Economic Development Council at the national level, and in the Economic Development Committees at industry level. And they should especially encourage dialogue and joint responsibility in dealing with cost-push inflation. But in the end it is government alone that has legitimate political authority, and government must have the final decision, which industry must respect.

8 "Render to Caesar"

ALTHOUGH RAISING TAXES is a matter of legislation rather than personal conduct, there are a number of reasons why it would be wrong to leave out the subject in this book. The state probably makes its greatest impact on most of us in its requirement that we pay to it a substantial proportion of our income, and a Christian's personal reaction to this requirement is important both to himself and others. Avoidance and evasion are widespread. A Christian must know the principle on which he himself should act, both in a personal capacity and in his official capacity as a trustee for others.

Personal problems apart, the system of taxation as we know it was devised at a time of strong Christian influence. The amount to be raised in taxes and the methods of raising it are based as much on moral principles as on administrative convenience. When people talk of the iniquitous burden of taxation or the justice of taxing those who can afford it, they are talking in moral terms and basing their views on moral principles. Taxation today is an instrument for the application of principles of work and wealth and social justice; if we do not want to find ourselves bound by law based on principles alien to our faith, it is as well that we should think out the place of Christian principles and uphold them as and when we have opportunity to do so. In any case, the world will judge us on our attitude toward these moral problems. The faith for which we are told by the apostle Paul to give reason is not confined to the doctrine of salvation, but includes doctrines of conduct and morality. These are questions we cannot and should not evade.

For a Christian there is no doubt about the absolute right of the state to raise taxes, whether those in power are democratically elected or an alien tyranny. We are told by our Lord to "render therefore to Caesar the things that are Caesar's," and He Himself set an example by paying His due tribute to the alien ruler. We are told in Romans 13 to render "taxes to whom taxes are due." The state is ordained by God and has certain rights over its citizens, of which this is one of the most important—important enough for specific instructions by our Lord Himself. In a democracy we do not even have the excuse put by the Jews, that it was wrong for the Lord's people to pay money to an alien tyrant.

MEETING A CITIZEN'S NEEDS

Some of a citizen's needs are met from payments by the state from tax revenue, and some directly from the individual's personal income. Where the line is drawn depends partly on custom and partly on moral principles. The cost of law and order and external defense has been met for so long by the state that it is hard to remember that powerful citizens once had private retainers who protected their interests and those of their dependents. Today many people feel that state spending has gone so far that it has sapped the moral fiber of the nation, but this extension was itself made on grounds of moral welfare. There is no doubt as to the Christian principle that the needs of the individual should be the first charge on his own family, and an individual Christian has no right to shove his responsibility onto the state as long as he is capable of meeting it himself. Similarly the church has an obligation to look after any of its members who are in genuine need. But if a family cannot or will not fulfill its responsibility, there is a strong case for saying that the other citizens, through the state, have a residual responsibility.

The state, like the family, is a divinely ordained institution, put there for the restraint of evil and the promotion of the common good of society. It does not need to administer the details of the life of a citizen to fulfill these aims. If voluntary bodies undertake the task, the state can withdraw. Its responsibility is fulfilled when it sees that what needs to be done is done by itself or by someone else. For instance, it is not necessary for the state to provide compensation for all those injured in car accidents. It is considered sufficient to see that all car owners themselves pay for insurance coverage and are heavily penalized if they do not. The state pension scheme in Britain is not compulsory, but the state requires that the employee be covered by a comparable scheme. To say that the state has a duty of care is not to say that it has a duty to tax and pay out in every detail of a citizen's life. But in some things, such as maintaining law and order, it is patently better, at least in society as it is today, for the state itself to administer.

In practice, boundaries of state expenditure have been set by the anxiety, on the one hand, that every citizen should have the right to vital goods and services (including education, housing, and medical care), and, on the other hand, that too much "laid on" regardless of individual effort will be bad for moral fiber. There is something in both points. Overanxiety for moral fiber led to the Victorian workhouse, and since that time the trend has been almost entirely the other way. But welfare service is now so universal that it has in turn attracted the weight of criticism. There is a feeling that the limit of public service has been reached and that, rather than a universal welfare state, there should be a welfare "safety net" to catch those in real want, leaving those who do not really require it to look after themselves. Various methods have been suggested for determining need without subjecting an individual to an unfair inquisition by strangers into his private affairs. The income tax gives a rough general guide to a person's means, though the numbers who do not pay tax, the loopholes that allow much income to go untaxed, and the fact that it covers only income and not wealth make this a less than satisfactory basis for determining eligibility for government subsidy of essential services. The Australian medical service is run on the basis that the patient has his medical fees refunded partly by the state and partly by compulsory medical benefit societies.

In medicine, the old practice of doctors providing free or low-cost services to the poor provided a safety net, but many who were poor but independent suffered rather than accept what they considered to be charity; and the practice depended entirely on the integrity of the individual doctor. Those who require the safety net are not all wage earners, capable of responding to a dose of moral fiber. A large proportion would be wives, children, and the very old. Any move away from free education could fall harshly on the able children of poor parents. The safety-net theory might control wasteful expenditure, but at some cost to the happiness of those who cannot look after themselves.

It seems logical to suppose that there must be some upper limit to the proportion of national income that can be taken in taxation, some point at which there is a sharply diminishing return for extra imposts. But one generation's predicted limit can seem absurdly low to the generation after. British government expenditure was 10 percent of the gross national product immediately before the First World War. Between the wars it rose to 20 percent, and since World War II it has varied between 36 and 40 percent. In 1910, when the House of Lords felt so strongly about increased taxation that it put its power and position at risk in the fight, the income tax was 9 percent, and the proposed supertax was to be 2.5 percent on incomes over £5,000 (which was equal to about $25,000 at then current exchange rates). In the United States, government expenditures were below 10 percent of the gross national product before World War I, rose to 20 percent during the Great Depression, was just over 20 percent after World War II, and has risen to 30–33 percent in recent years.

THE LIMITS OF TAXATION

Perhaps a better guide than moral indignation is the growth of avoidance and evasion. Beyond a certain point, taxable income disappears either through legal avoidance or illegal evasion. Although tax rates are now lower in both Britain and the U.S. than they were immediately after the war, there is some evidence that a high level of taxes sustained for so long has begun this process. No one can be complacent about this, particularly since avoidance and evasion bring the rule of law itself into contempt. If the rule of law, which is the basis of an ordered society, is to be maintained, then legislation must have general support. It is this requirement which, in the world as it is, places a practical limit on the extent to which people's affairs can be subjected to legislation. If we find that taxation beyond a certain level brings a high degree of avoidance and evasion, then that is a guide to the practical upper limit of taxation.

The quickest solution to the need to finance a growing level of public expenditure would be a proportionate or more rapid rise in national taxable income. This would pay for the expenditure without extra taxes. But in the long run it may be necessary to find some way in which to reinvigorate the check on public expenditure that used to be exercised to some effect by the legislature.

Adam Smith laid down four famous canons of taxation: (1) Taxation should be equal (on equal incomes) or proportional to income; (2) Tax levies should not be uncertain or arbitrary; (3) Taxes should not be exacted in an inconvenient manner; (4) Taxes should be economical to collect. It is interesting to note that the first two, which are the most important, have a moral basis. In fact, almost any general principle of taxation must be established on grounds such as fairness, justice, and duty. A Christian would probably accept the principle that taxation should be equal, in the sense that all taxpayers in similar circumstances should bear an equal tax burden. If we are to love our neighbors as ourselves, we should not wish him to bear a burden which, in similar circumstances, we would not be prepared to bear ourselves. This principle means that every distinction in the tax structure should have some reasonable justification and be fair as between taxpayers. It also means that loopholes creating artificial distinctions should be closed by legislation as they become evident. Tax concepts such as "income" and "earned income" should be defined accurately, realistically, and truthfully.

Whereas it was necessary for Adam Smith in his day to argue that taxes should be proportional to income (i.e., the rate of tax should be equal), the present principle is that taxes should be progressive (i.e., at an increasing rate for increasing incomes). There are arguments against progressive taxation, but they are not always as strong as they seem. Progressive taxation may have been a major factor in increasing the level of gross salaries, since the steep differentials in the higher ranges would not seem functionally necessary except for providing noticeable net differentials. Even where they are functionally necessary they often reflect the shortage of a particular skill rather than extra training or responsibility, and progressive taxes take back for the community something of the extra amount made by the person who has temporarily "cornered" that skill. However, it is one thing to accept progression as a general principle and another to agree with a very high rate of progression. Steep progression on income places an effective ceiling on income and is equivalent to saying that no one—however skilled or responsible, however hazardous his job, or however temporary the income—deserves to earn more than so much in a year. This is not a proposition that most people would defend as fair, and it is certainly one that no union negotiator, arguing on differentials, would accept for a moment.

If there is to be progressive taxation, it would seem fairer to put a levy on expenditure rather than on income. Instead of saying that no one *deserves* more than so much a year, the law would be saying that no one *needs* more than so much a year, which would surely seem to be more susceptible to objective judgment. And if it is not possible to judge objectively about a person's needs, it is certainly not possible to judge what he deserves. Not only would such a tax seem to be fairer, but the moral case also seems stronger. It is surely better to tax someone on what he takes out of the community than on what he puts into it. The effect of the present system is to treat accumulated wealth lightly, but to tax new savings heavily. This freezes society into its present stratification and increases the dependence of wage and salary earners on those who have inherited accumulated wealth. It would seem more just to tax new savings relatively lightly and to put the weight on expenditure and on large accumulations and transfers of wealth. Luxurious spending takes a disproportionate and unnecessary share of goods and services; it is both depraving and a social evil. An expenditure tax at a lower rate of progression than the present income tax rates in Britain (which is much higher than the rate of progression in the U.S.), would effectively reform the present inequities. Roughly speaking, annual expenditure would be arrived at by deducting the year's increase in assets from income or adding the decrease to income.

ATTEMPTING MORAL EQUITY

The feasibility of this kind of expenditure tax has been expounded by Nicholas Kaldor in his book *An Expenditure Tax*. Its main requirement is an annual declaration of capital as well as of income, but this has to be done to some extent for capital gains taxes and is done at present in the Scandinavian countries for their capital taxes. It might also require some averaging of exceptional expenditure, but this should be no more complex than the present fairly simple rules for averaging exceptional income. Combined with wealth transfer taxes, this would allow all saving during a person's lifetime to be exempt from high rates of tax, but would effectively break up large accumulations of capital. As with so many attempts at moral equity, it does add some complication; but if moral equity is what people want—and it is what we want—then the additional complications are a small price to pay.

Some measure of redistribution of capital would seem to be in accordance with the Christian view of wealth discussed earlier. While great wealth may be used to good purpose, it may also be used to exploit or to exercise power over others and may be used for ostentatious display that can only aggravate social conflict. Redistribution does not, it must be granted, add much to the wealth of the many, for the very reason that they are many and the great fortunes are spread over the few. But it may well be that what is added is of more significance to the poor man, woman, or child who gains it than the rich person who gives it up. Any marginal increase in income matters a lot to anyone living at or about subsistence level. It also matters a lot to a backward country, trying to make the first economic advances, where it may well raise its people above subsistence level.

There are limits to redistribution. If we follow the logic of our earlier arguments, it should not go so far as to subject the proceeds of taxes to the law of diminishing returns. It should be aimed against the accumulation over generations of powerful fortunes rather than hamper the creation of wealth by taking away from someone each year most of what his own efforts have earned him in that year. Labor and reward are linked in Christian teaching, and tax structures should not be so extreme as virtually to destroy this association.

Taxation has not been used only for social redistribution. It has also traditionally been used to dampen certain types of expenditure where excess has been considered socially undesirable. This has been done by high flat-rate sales taxes, mainly on alcoholic beverages and tobacco. There is little doubt that cheap gin was a social disaster. "Drunk for a penny, dead drunk for twopence, clean straw free" was a slogan that reflected real conditions in Britain. Hogarth drew from life and not from imagination. Evidence about the effects of cigarette smoking puts it into a similar category. At the other end of the scale, there has always been a strong reluctance to impose taxes on food. Both these positions seem basically right. On the other hand, as the late Sir Gerald Nabarro demonstrated in a series of detailed questions in the House of Commons, the system of varied rates of tax, classing some goods as luxuries and others as essentials, can be made to look very silly and smacks rather too much of bureaucratic paternalism for most people's liking. One of the advantages of a progressive expenditure tax instead of high personal tax is that it would have the desired social effect without the paternalism and absurdity of differential rates of taxes on expenditure.

Most countries place more emphasis on flat-rate taxes on expenditure, such as sales or value-added taxes, than on general taxes on income. The argument for them is that they are easier to assess and more difficult to evade. There is a further argument: they can be used more precisely than income taxes to control inflationary and deflationary cycles in the economy. The main moral objection to them is that they are regressive (i.e., the less income you have, the higher the proportion you pay in tax); moreover, if they are to include necessities like food, this is a definite objection. It is in principle, as we have argued, more just to tax expenditure than income—to tax someone on what he takes out rather than what he puts in. But the case for this tax is not so strong as for the progressive expenditure tax on individuals. As lower incomes rise and the regressive effects of such a tax matter less, the case will become stronger; but at the moment the pros and cons are nicely balanced.

THE RIGHT TO AVOID TAXES

As far as tax evasion is concerned, for a Christian there is no problem: It is illegal, and he must not do it. The problems arise from what is called "avoidance," which is the arrangement of one's affairs in such a way as to minimize liability to tax. This is a citizen's legal right. It is expressed in a number of legal judgments. Lord Clyde, a Scottish judge, has said,

> No man in this country is under the smallest obligation, legal or other, so to arrange his legal relations to his business or to his property as to enable the Inland Revenue to put the largest possible shovel into his stores. The Inland Revenue is not slow—and quite rightly—to take every advantage which is open to it under the taxing statutes for the purpose of depleting the taxpayer's pocket. And the taxpayer is, in like manner, entitled to be astute to prevent, so far as he honestly can, the depletion of his means by the Inland Revenue.

In a leading House of Lords decision, Lord Sumner said,

> My Lords, the highest authorities have always recognized that the subject is entitled to arrange his affairs as not to attract taxes imposed by the Crown so far as he can do so within the law, and that he may legitimately claim the advantage of any express terms or of any omission that he can find in his favour in the taxing acts. In doing so, he neither comes under liability nor incurs blame.

This is the law in both Britain and the United States. It is expressly recognized that there is no measure of fairness—what the law calls equity—in taxation. You are either in the letter of the statute and liable, or outside and not liable. You cannot be excluded by pleading equity (the technical term for natural justice), and you cannot, therefore, be included by an Internal Revenue plea of equity. The principle of equity applies to other branches of the law, but not to taxation.

This is not, however, quite the end of the matter. While it would be wrong to ask the Christian to set himself up as a judge on the fairness or unfairness of a point of law, he cannot proceed without the slightest recognition of the difference between various classes of avoidance or of the general effects of avoidance. That there are differences is recognized in a judgment by Lord Simon, when he was Lord Chancellor.

> My Lords, of recent years much ingenuity has been expended in certain quarters to devise methods of disposition of income by which those who were prepared to adopt them might enjoy the benefits of residence in this country while

> receiving the equivalent of such income without sharing in the appropriate burden of British taxation. Judicial dicta may be cited which point out that however elaborate and artificial such methods may be, those who adopt them are 'entitled' to do so. There is, of course, no doubt that they are within their legal rights, but that is no reason why their efforts, or those of the professional gentlemen who assist them in the matter, should be regarded as commendable exercise of ingenuity or as a discharge of the duties of good citizenship. On the contrary, one result of such methods, if they succeed is, of course, to increase pro tanto the load of tax on the shoulders of the great body of good citizens, who do not desire, or do not know how, to adopt these manoeuvres.

There is a difference, for instance, between using an Independent Retirement Account (IRA) to spread income into retirement, when it will be taxed at a lower rate, and systematic operation of the complex procedures that attempt to convert ordinary income into more lightly taxed capital gains through tax shelters. The one is taking advantage of a provision clearly intended for the purpose, the other is like driving a horse and cart through an accidental loophole. Few reasonable people would interpret the latter as being in the spirit of the law. All the transactions are highly artificial, and the provisions are being used for a purpose for which they were never intended.

There is another principle that a Christian can bring to bear in doubtful cases. This is that he should earn his living in a way befitting to a Christian. His livelihood should have some constructive purpose, and spending his whole life in finding loopholes in the tax laws hardly fits this bill. There is a clear distinction between the work of the normal accountant who advises his clients on their tax and the person whose reputation depends on his skill in working out methods of sailing as close to the wind as possible.

The author was asked in the late sixties to investigate the possibility of introducing a Value Added Tax in Britain. When he asked the Germans about their rate of evasion of VAT, they maintained that every German, faced with a tax form, would fill it in correctly and that there was no evasion. Not believing this totally, they were reported as having 5 percent evasion. In a neighboring country, the shoulder-shrugging answer to the same question was, "If we knew that we would collect the tax." They were put down as having 20 percent evasion.

The country's taxation depends to a greater degree than we would like to admit on tax morality. But tax morality also depends on the burden of tax. Since a Christian maintains absolutely the obligation to pay the full tax liability, he is much concerned about evasion. Shoulder-shrugging acceptance of a high degree of evasion puts a particularly heavy burden on those who determinedly pay the full whack. There is little argument that very high taxes increase the rate of evasion, and indeed the main sign that taxes are too high is the development of a "black" cash economy with a rise in moonlighting second jobs. While a Christian may agree with the principles of redistribution, he will recognize that it is not feasible beyond a certain point and that, if pressed beyond this point, the tax yield will actually drop and the country's tax morality will suffer.

It is partly for this reason that a Christian regards redistribution by law to absolute equality of incomes as unpractical. The Christian can set standards for himself, and he can try in a materialistic society to be an example to others. But it is no part of Christian principles that these standards should be imposed on every other citizen by penal taxation or redistributive incomes policies. The rich young ruler was asked to give his wealth voluntarily to the poor; when he was evidently too attached to his riches, Christ did not go to the Romans to suggest that they should levy a wealth tax and do the job by force. And it is not only an unselfish desire for equality, but greed and envy that are behind the desire to impose penal taxes.

A Christian should aim instead for a society in which vast inequalities of wealth and income are considered intolerable and in which any legislation to reduce those inequalities has broad popular support among both rich and poor alike.

9 Fair Trading

There is a strong trend today in Britain toward more competitive industry, and Britain's situation in the world is such that this is unlikely to be reversed. At the same time, there is a good deal of ignorance about what competition really means. Most people think of it as price competition, but there is competition also in advertising, design, and sheer persuasion. Even price competition is not straightforward. In the United States, where competition has long been held to be to the general benefit of society, a mass of legislation has been necessary to try to impose this simple concept in the vast variety of different situations that arise. Despite this formidable effort, few industrialists there seem to feel that the legislation is entirely fair even now in meeting the complexities of price competition. But competition is held to be a major check on the power of capitalism, and anyone attempting to moralize must find out what it is and what it does.

This simple theory of price competition is that the manufacturer who can make a product cheaper than the next person's is entitled to sell it more cheaply and thereby to gain a larger share of the business. This helps to keep down the cost of goods, and it works to the public benefit in stimulating the growth of the more efficient firms.

The difficulty is that in practice the situation is almost always more complicated than this. Today costs are increasingly incurred not in payment of wages for daily output, but in the original installation of plant and machinery. This is the difference between variable cost and sunk cost. The higher the sunk cost, the greater the gulf between the average cost of production over a period of time and the cost of producing a marginal extra unit. In some very highly capitalized industries, the average cost can be 80 percent of selling price, giving an average profit of 20 percent; the marginal cost of an extra unit can be as low as 10 percent, giving a marginal profit of 90 percent. Here low costs depend as much on volume as on efficiency, and volume may well depend in turn almost solely on price.

In these circumstances, the temptation is to keep a high price to the majority of customers and to gain extra business by price-cutting (in a limited section of the market). In the United States, this is regarded as unfair practice, and the general rule is that the seller should charge customers the same for the same product. But even this simple rule is hard to enforce, because the law allows a company to reduce the price to match a competitor's price rather than break its price structure or lose the business. This permits sellers to have one price for one customer and another price for another customer. It then becomes very difficult to tell who is making competition and who is matching it.

THE DIFFICULTY OF CONTROL

The fact of life is that it is very hard to control a flexible and fluid pricing situation with an inflexible instrument like legislation. This is not to deny that some sort of protection is necessary. Companies cannot only be unfair as between their customers, but a large and powerful company can use differential pricing to discriminate against a particular competitor, cutting prices on the products made by the competitor either to bring it to heel or even to run it out of business. To control this situation requires, not the dead hand of statute law and legal precedent, but someone well informed on the economics of the industry and capable of holding the ring. An impartial arbiter could also deal with genuine cases where lower costs give an advantage to some companies and put the future of their competitors at risk.

Very often an industry holds up prices in order to protect the weaker companies. No individual company has a particular responsibility to lay plans that would enable the industry to work its way out of such a situation; and even if one company did put up plans, it might not be powerful enough to gain acceptance of its solution. The more one goes into the matter, the more the assumption that unsupervised competition will bring about the best possible result appears as a doctrinaire view based on long-outdated premises. It may have been appropriate to deal with an industry with many producers with low capitalization, but not with a few large companies with high capitalization. Today it is not so much the survival of the fittest as the survival of the fattest.

While there is no referee to competition, a Christian who is in a position to decide trading policies will have to work out his own solutions as best he may. His guiding rule is the old one that he should treat others with the respect he would like to receive from them. On the other hand, while unfettered competition is the rule, he cannot concede a competitive advantage. If competition is tough, he will have to be tough too. But if he has any influence in his industry, it should be exercised in a constructive way, to achieve what he thinks a fair solution—not only for the industry, but also for its customers. For example, he should not be content with a price policy that gives him a reasonable reward if the policy still allows customers to suffer from discriminatory pricing.

Where there is price competition, the profits that can be obtained will be governed by the competitive price level. But there are still times at which it will be necessary to set some objective standard for prices and profits. This is particularly the case in bringing out a new product. There is, of course, the cheerful, unworried businessman whose philosophy is "all the market will bear." But aside from the social repercussions, this is not usually good business unless the company is going to shut down in the near future. High profits are likely in fairly quick time to attract competition, and in highly capitalized industries this can result in formidable overcapacity for a prolonged period.

Assuming that the costs of a product can be properly allocated, the factors in fixing the price are the price of money (the interest on capital), the capital/output ratio (the relation between capital employed and the level of output of the product) and the risk factor (the risk over time of obsolescence of plant and product). These factors require a profit margin on unit price higher than most people outside industry will credit. To the outsider, an industry may appear solidly established, even formidable in its dominance of the market. The person who has to stay in business in a competitive world, and who realizes the dependence of his work force on his decisions, sees the world as a much more hazardous place.

Perhaps the most controversial factor in the level of company profits is not so much the risk factor—which no one with industrial experience will dispute—but the extent to which the company should use the profit revenue from its current products to finance its movement into other activities, instead of paying out to stockholders, customers, and work force. Certainly there is a tendency on the part of companies to hang onto more money than is strictly necessary, and it is easy to see in the extreme cases that this is wrong. But the pattern of business does change over time, and the increasing rate of techncial innovation requires a sufficient investment in research at least to keep abreast of change. It also requires sufficient cash in hand to get through a competitive rough spell when it may not be possible to find money on the market. Nor can a new product go on the market without teething troubles. The more highly capitalized the industry, the less likely the new product will be to recover its costs quickly. For a time new products have to be subsidized through profits on products whose costs have been reduced through long experience in manufacture. Profitability cannot really be assessed except over a period of years, and there have to be fat years to make up for the lean before price and margin are reduced as more competitors move into the field. In some industries, where only a proportion of projects will get off the ground, those that do go well have to pay for those that do not.

Pricing is only one part of industrial competition. In intercompany selling, decisions are increasingly made on design, specifications, and general confidence in performance. The decision of individuals in the buying company can be of vital importance, and the knowledge that two or three individuals can be decisive in the placing of a multimillion-dollar order would seem to place strenuous demands on integrity as well as salesmanship.

CONCERN FOR THE TRUTH

A Christian's concern for the truth must be paramount, and it might seem at first sight that there would be a conflict between his obligation to be truthful and his desire to persuade the buyer. But this is not usually the problem it seems. Almost all industrial purchases are intended for a purpose. The purpose commonly requires a specification, and the specification is a matter of objective measurement. The seller knows perfectly well that if his machine is not up to specification it will be returned. There are, of course, claims that can be made on the margin, but a sophisticated industrial buyer is likely to know as much about his subject as the seller; if he is any good at all, he is unlikely to sign multimillion-dollar contracts—or indeed contracts for any amount—through misunderstanding as to what he is buying.

Apart from any moral standards, enlightened self-interest is likely to keep the seller to the truth. He will want to make and preserve his company's reputation. He will want the customer to come again, and the customer is unlikely to do this if he has been sold any species of pup. This is the kind of area in business where "honesty is the best policy." It is not, therefore, an area where a Christian should find himself in a serious moral dilemma. There are matters that do not go to the root of the contract where a Christian should earn a reputation as a man of his word. In the best-ordered businesses, there will be late deliveries. There will be strikes and unscheduled breakdowns against which there can be no guarantee. But a Christian should be as fair and accurate as he can be in giving delivery dates. He should not consistently obtain business on the basis of delivery dates that are unlikely to be kept, and if there is some known hazard about delivery, he should say so.

A Christian who looks after his company's interests will be a tough negotiator. But there is a difference in people's minds between *hard bargaining,* which is considered fair, and *hard bargains,* which are not. A Christian should not earn the reputation of squeezing the last ounce out of every situation. This much, at least, should be deduced from the parable of the unforgiving steward, who, having been forgiven a major debt by his lord, was merciless in exacting a much smaller debt that someone else owed to him (Matt. 18:21–35). It can be deduced, too, from biblical teaching on usury, the essence of which is that we should not take advantage of the temporary weakness of our neighbor. For instance, if a contract is entered into in good faith and circumstances arise that were not envisioned by either party, it is fairer to renegotiate than to press your legal rights to the detriment of the other party. The best business practice is that one should "not be too greedy" and should always try to leave something in it for the other person. The person who wants to preserve a reputation in the business world takes care never to leave a bad taste behind and bears in mind that there is always another day and another deal. The Christian standard should certainly be no less than this.

Another aspect of this question is the amounts that should be spent in entertaining customers. A Christian should hardly need to discuss the worst abuses of expense accounts. Putting in for more than he has spent, with or without the connivance of his firm, is a fraud, if not on the firm, then certainly on the Internal Revenue Service. There is no question about this: We are told to be honest and that is an end of the matter. Nor is there any problem in the entertainment of friends under guise of customers: This too is wrong.

The problem for a Christian lies in the amount and kind of entertainment he should provide for genuine customers. Having a meal with a customer is in itself right and proper. We have to get to know the people with whom we are doing business, and an invitation to eat together is both a gesture of friendliness and an opportunity for better acquaintance. The abuse begins when the level of entertainment goes beyond what we would do for personal friends. When entertainment is at a higher level than someone would expect, it begins to move away from the line that preserves the strict impartiality of the officer of the purchasing company. Taking a junior purchasing officer out to dinner in the smartest of nightspots either affects his judgment, in which case it is wrong, or it does not affect it, in which case it is a waste of the company's money.

It may be difficult to decide the exact level of entertainment appropriate to a particular customer, but it should not be impossible. The British Foreign Office has arrived over the years at a workable arrangement for different levels of entertainment. A fair guide is the standard of living of the giver and receiver of the hospitality. What would be a pleasant memento to a wealthy director could well be a bribe to an assistant purchasing officer. Conversely, the hospitality expected from the chairman of a company is bound to be greater than that offered by an individual salesman. What would seem wrong is the giving of entertainment at expensive establishments by individuals who would never dream of incurring this sort of bill on their own account for their friends or family. This is what the man in the street means when he complains of businessmen who are "living it up on expense account."

BUSINESS WITHOUT BRIBERY

It is just a short step from this to outright bribery. The Bible clearly and specifically condemns giving gifts to judges; although bribing a judge of law is more serious than bribing someone who has to judge between different bids, the principle would seem to be the same. Fortunately it is still possible to stay in business in our own country without bribery, although the Christian should be aware of the dangers and use his influence to maintain high standards of integrity. All of us tend to underestimate our own influence, but a Christian especially should have some faith that if he acts as he should, his actions will not be ineffective.

The real problem, however, comes in exporting to countries where little or no business can be transacted without gifts. Should a Christian avoid all business in these countries? There are degrees of gifts. There are those clearly intended to influence business. On the other hand, there are those which are accepted by certain people as a supplementary salary in countries where civil servants are not given a living wage. These take the form of a local tax or toll. They are paid to the clerk for prompt clearance of documents; to the secretary for an appointment to see the cabinet official; to the harbormaster for seeing goods through customs in reasonable time. These are all gifts on a small scale, do not pervert judgment, and are known to the local government; the amounts payable are said to be obtainable, in many cases, from the local consular officers. It would seem to be slightly dogmatic to condemn all those who make this sort of payment, but for the sake of integrity of local expatriate staff, it is desirable that these payments should be paid by the local agent out of his normal commission.

The opening up of world trade and the fall of regimes that were colonial but honest have raised the problems of bribery much more acutely. It is not enough to say, as some companies do, that these are customs which are a local way of life and that exporters must go along with them. Every country's laws condemn these very local customs, and at every coup d'état and certainly at every revolution, those who defrauded their community are condemned, exiled, imprisoned, or shot. It is just as well for the expatriate not to be caught up in this process. Nor can a company draw a *cordon sanitaire* between its own staff and those receiving bribes. What is sauce for the goose is sauce for the gander. Who is to say that those who hand on the bribes are not taking a cut for themselves? And if the company is known to be paying bribes, it will very soon find that its own local staff are being offered bribes. In the case of very big orders, these can be very big bribes—enough to tempt someone to forget his loss of salary, pension, and professional reputation when he is discovered.

Yet the pressures are very great. In the great majority of cases—to which the notorious Lockheed case seems to have been an exception—bribes are not paid to pervert judgment to enable the company to knock out a competitor, but because all bidders have been told that to qualify for the tender there must be an addition to the bid price of 2½ or 5 or 10 percent payable to a nominated intermediary, and no bid without this addition will be considered. The company has to reckon the loss in employment if it absolutely refuses to bid in the very large number of countries when these conditions exist. It was recently reckoned to cover about a quarter of Europe's export markets, and absolute refusal of all export companies to trade would cost millions of jobs.

Some companies nevertheless refuse to trade under these conditions. At the height of the Lockheed affair, the author was sitting at lunch next to the president of a major American company who volunteered that he was not going to risk a summons to testify in Washington no matter what orders his company lost as a result. The author knows another multinational which issues a direction to its worldwide affiliates that no "extracontractual" payments of any amount, however small, were to be made by the company by anyone at all to anyone at all for any reason at all. A European multinational once made a similar decision, and it was so vital to the economy of most countries in which it operated that it was allowed to carry on regardless. However, in one country, after the usual coup d'état, the company was told by the new regime—bent on discrediting the old—that if it owned up to the payments it had made to the old regime, all would be forgiven. After a strenuous audit by senior officials from Europe, the multinational reported that no payments could be discovered; but bribery was so common that the new regime refused to believe their report, and the multinational had considerable difficulty in re-establishing good relations.

It is not impossible to refuse. It is in the interests of those who demand bribes to create an atmosphere in which international business is persuaded that they have to be paid, and it is also in their interests to talk up the going rate. However, those who demand bribes live in a perilous world in which discovery can end forever the capacity to extort. So it is in the interests of international business to create a counter-atmosphere, to hint that on the refusal of their bid, the whole tender may well become notorious and this would embarrass their government and lead to inquiries. Companies who do not believe they are in the class that enables them to fight extortion head-on tend to rely on their local agents and look to them to meet any costs out of their regular agents' commissions. The agent judges the minimum payment he can get away with in the local circumstances, and the company is not involved. But when the greed of the extortioners raises the standard percentage demanded, the agent is forced to go back to the company to tell them that he cannot meed the demands out of his commission. When this happens, the agent may also worry that the whole process is becoming notorious and may refuse to handle any more payments, throwing the responsibility back onto the company.

THE PROBLEM OF CORRUPTION

The international business community has become increasingly concerned with the problem of corruption. They were angry at the unprovoked competitive bribery by American aircraft manufacturers that encouraged a surge of demands on them well beyond the capacity of their agents to meet. They felt themselves caught between government's pressure to export and government's condemnation of extracontractual payments, where a cabinet official could one day make a speech demanding that such payments should all stop at once and three days later entertain and honor officially the very overseas customers who were making the most outrageous demands for extracontractual payments.

As chairman of the British Overseas Trade Board at this time, the author was at the chief point of contact between the government and the exporting industry in Britain and did what he could to bring the problems into frank discussion. Both government and industry had the strongest reasons for discouraging corrupt practices, and it seemed sensible that there should be a constructive dialogue about what might be done.

Since a sharp difference of approach between the Americans and the Europeans had emerged, the author also met with those responsible for drafting American legislation. The United States exports only 8 percent of its national product, and of this a large part is agricultural; so industry exports only a fractional percentage, which is not as vital to the economy as it is in European industry, where 20 to 30 percent of production is exported. So the United States proposed to make illegal American companies' breaches of the corruption laws of other countries, even though the laws are not enforced in the countries themselves. This legislation would also operate extraterritorially on all American-affiliated companies overseas. Since America could afford to lose the business more easily than Europe, and since the European Community resented the existing extraterritorial jurisdiction of America, this solution was not well thought of in Europe.

In addition, Europe does not have such a strong tradition of resorting to legislation. Rather, it has a much stronger tradition of voluntary cooperation between companies. So it is more rational for European companies to come to informal agreements that they will consult each other about pressure for noncontractual payments with a view to resisting them. Behind this there is now an agreement by the International Chamber of Commerce on a code of practice; it has a high-level committee in which complaints can be made about companies breaching the code. It may be that this code—which covers all major trading countries—will prove inadequate because companies cannot trust each other to keep it. In that case the European Community should consider legislation and should make a major attempt to persuade Japan, Canada, and other major trading nations to introduce parallel legislation. The aim must be to reduce to negligible proportions the number of bidders who are prepared to yield to pressure for extracontractual payments and to make notorious those contracts where demands are made and the countries that condone them. Concerted action by the major industrial countries can give their exporters the confidence to resist their demands.

THE NEED FOR TRUST

In one way or another corruption has to be curtailed. Our highly complex industrial society depends on trust, and corruption destroys that trust. The stockholders have to trust the directors, and the depositors have to trust the banks. Auditors can check honest companies to make sure no dishonesty has crept in, but if most companies become dishonest, an army of auditors could not put it right. And in a dishonest society, who knows whether even the auditor does not have his price? In a dishonest and corrupt society no one trusts anyone except maybe his son or brother or nephew, who are subject to harsh disciplines if they deceive their own family. In corrupt societies professors demand payment for degrees, so only foreign degrees are a reliable guide to technical competence. No one knows whether his buyer has been bought, whether his salesmen are being bribed by a competitor, whether his accountant is being bribed to extend credit, whether his negotiators are taking a rake-off themselves. So nothing is taken on trust, and business is small-scale, slow, and uncertain.

If corruption undermines trust in industrial society, it will collapse. Individuals as well as companies and governments must do all they can to resist it. Managers must avoid companies that do not have the kind of standards with which they can work, and they must be prepared to move elsewhere at a loss if acceptable standards are broken.

Directors must not turn a blind eye to what is done in their name, but must insist on knowing what is done to obtain orders and what precautions are being taken against corruption. This may mean diversifying their trade away from countries where corruption is endemic and making a major effort to build new business in countries where markets are tough but honest.

The citizen must recognize that corruption is a real problem and must not—by underpaying public servants, police, and others in positions of trust—tempt them to betray that trust. Britain obtained an incorrupt judiciary by recognzing that it was wise to value their judges as highly as those who were trying to bribe them. In the end, the individual manager or director has to consider whether he is prepared to risk his whole professional reputation and future in making, authorizing, or condoning an extracontractual payment. Arguments that sound plausible in the boardroom have a very different sound in front of a congressional or parliamentary committee. Those of us who have seen the isolation and humiliation of formerly respected public figures smeared by association with corruption will not easily forget it. A Christian above all must maintain the absolutely incorrupt private standards and public reputation that are expected of him.

But apart from bribery, it is part of a salesman's job to use his powers of persuasion. There is nothing to be ashamed of in trying to convince a potential customer of the genuine merits of your product. But a salesman who has Christian standards sets himself limits. First, is a Christian's absolute obligation not to tell lies; this includes both what he says and what he infers. He cannot tell everything about his goods, but what he omits must not make what he says misleading. Second, a Christian must remember that his customer is a man created by God as a rational being and must be respected as such; we should appeal, therefore, to his reason and not to his subconscious. Third, we must, particularly in personal encounter, respect the dignity and integrity of a man's personality; it is wrong for a strong personality to ride roughshod over a weaker one.

A manufacturer is faced with the facts of mass production and the consequent need of a mass market. As living standards rise and necessities take a lower proportion of income, an increasing proportion of manufacturing output goes into producing goods that people can buy or stop buying as they fancy. Consumer spending becomes more flexible. But in parallel, high living standards are brought about by higher capitalization, and this makes production less flexible. There are, therefore, the strongest possible pressures on businessmen to secure both uniformity and continuity by standardizing demand and securing their customers' allegiance. Added to these pressures is our social desire to give people a choice and therefore to maintain competition between different manufacturers of the same product. These are the key factors in the rise of advertising.

THE COST OF ADVERTISING

Before judging too hastily on the "waste" expenditure of advertising, it is as well to look behind the very high absolute figures. If there were no advertising this amount of money would not be saved; newspapers, magazines, and everything else subsidized by advertising would probably cost twice as much. Nevertheless, even allowing for this—and for some brightness, zest, and significance which good advertising can give to some of the chores of life—the cost in time and talent is undoubtedly high. Industry spends twice as much on advertising as on research. Both on social and economic grounds it is probably right to try to keep advertising within bounds. It is not always easy to see how this can be done. If a product is the subject of competitive advertising and one firm cuts its advertising budget, it will almost certainly lose market share. The best method for a Christian who thinks that advertising expenditure in his own industry is excessive and wasteful is to try to work with his competitors for a mutual reduction in the level (albeit this might be illegal under antitrust laws in the United States).

Although there are obvious dangers in advertising, there is no need, in measuring them, to accept the advertising industry's own assessment of its effectiveness at face value. It is true that anyone who takes the trouble to think about the matter will, because he is accustomed to think, be less likely to be affected much by advertising; but even discounting this, there is evidence that the effectiveness of advertising on the human will is overstated. It is true that in competitive advertising, brand-switching is responsive to advertising volume; but what worries most people, particularly Christians, is not so much the plugging of brand names as the pressure of appeals to the worst traits in human nature, like avarice and arrogance. If these appeals were uniformly successful, we would be entitled to be worried. But the fact is, people are a good deal less subject to pressure than advertisers will admit.

In America in the late fifties, there was enormous spending by all the major auto manufacturers on advertising cars, which were larger, longer, more prestigious, and more powerful. To own last year's model was said to lead to social disaster. In fact, the cars that increased their share of the market most rapidly were the small imported cars with small engines and few trimmings, and the most popular was the Volkswagen—which had not changed its basic style since the 1930s. (It is fair to note, however, that at that time even Volkswagen did not capture a very large share of the total U.S. market, which was still greatly dominated by the domestic carmakers.) Social prestige went to the owner of the imported sports car which had much less prestige build-up through advertising. The subject of one of the largest market research and promotional expenditures in automobile history—the Edsel—was a complete flop. In Britain, BMC (now BL) produced a small estate-car and gave it the very utilitarian title of the Morris Traveller, with the market for commercial travelers clearly in mind. It was very successful, not least as a second car for upper-income families who were not in the least put off by its name. If we are discussing the morality of advertising pressure, we may be discussing what people are trying to do. It does not follow that they are succeeding.

The other point worth making before we start to moralize is that most advertising is concerned with a straightforward description of the goods advertised. Almost all technical advertising falls into this category. So does a great deal of advertising of consumer goods. Most clothing advertisements, for instance, have little more than a drawing or photograph, a price and a very brief description. There are few moral problems here, provided the descriptions are not misleading; and, unless one thinks that people are really misled by the slight poetic license, most descriptions would seem to be reasonable.

The moral problem begins to arise as one moves into the area where the real differences between competing products are significant. This includes the products of process industries that cannot be described except in technical terms unintelligible to the layperson. Gasoline and laundry detergents are examples. There seems to be two different paths which companies can take. One is simply to concentrate on some positive identification of the product—a hallmark that associates the advertisement with the product at the point of sale, but need hardly bother with a description. One of the best is the British prewar "That's Shell that was" that survived in folklore long after it was dropped by the company (which went on to the more mundane "You can be sure of Shell"). An American example is Texaco's "You can trust your car to the man who wears the star."

The other line, which seems less desirable but hardly more effective, is to try to associate the product with some mood or attitude of the buyer. The advertiser tries to make the reader identify himself with the man or woman in the advertisement who is using the product, and the type of person projected is, not unnaturally, very much a man or woman of the world. As one British critic puts it, "Advertisement man is an urban good-looker with one unmistakable virtue, ambition. He is clearly on the way up, a coming top person, outstripping his fellows all the way along in clothes, girls, cars, and cigarettes. He is a conformist, permanently inoculated against awkward critical hesitations or doubts." On the other hand, many people's instinctive reaction against all the smug men in the advertisements is hostility rather than awe. Whether these ads really have a more sinister effect on any but the weakest minds is open to argument.

THE OPPORTUNITIES OF INGENUITY

A Christian who has any say in advertising policy will almost certainly want to avoid advertisements that are undisguised appeals to covetousness or are based on erotic appeal. But such is the range of human ingenuity that this ought not to cramp his style. He will also want to exercise the greatest care in the field of patent medicine. This is subject to legal restrictions, but there is probably a gray area within the letter of the law where claims, unless qualified, could be misleading.

In *The Hidden Persuaders,* Vance Packard has illuminated the dangers of a lack of respect for human personality in advertising. Some of the reported advice given by psychologists and motivational research men appears to be nothing but sound common sense. For instance, there is little in their reputed advice on the unfortunate "image" of the California prune that is likely to worry a Christian. But their attitude toward people is disturbing. The industrialist realizes that his ability to stay in business partly depends on the irrational whims of the buyer, and a desire to guard against these irrationalities has led some companies to get advice from psychologists.

Yet it is one thing to defend yourself against irrationalities; it is quite a different affair to exploit them. There is no doubt that people do have an "image" of a company or a product, and this may be quite irrational. For instance, one understands that the traditional delicate lettering of Rolls-Royce—which made no difference in Britain where a favorable "image" was long-established—was quite unsuitable in South America and had to be replaced by a much more rugged lettering. This kind of image-building seems to be quite harmless. But if advertising can latch onto some subconscious urge and persuade families to buy useless status symbols on long installment terms, it is both misusing human knowledge and disregarding the dignity of man as a rational being. As Vance Packard expresses his own attitude, he does not claim that he is never irrational, but if he is going to be irrational he wants to decide himself and not have a stranger decide for him.

A Christian is likely to be at a disadvantage when he is faced by competitors' claims that he does not think it right to match. The more such claims can be cut down to size, the more the honest trade will benefit. The only question about the various attempts to bring some standards and objective judgment into the field of consumer buying is whether they do their job effectively. There are various voluntary industry standards and tests by independent groups, such as Underwriters Laboratories, with their accompanying seals of approval. There is some legislation on descriptions. There are roadtests in auto magazines that carry advertising for the same cars, but whose warnings are perfectly clear to the practiced reader: "On the model tested, the brakes did not work. We understand that this has been rectified on subsequent models.'' Finally, in recent years there have come the consumers' tests, with the forthright *Which?,* magazine of the Consumers' Association in Britain, and *Consumer Reports, The Magazine of Consumers Union,* in America, well in the lead. These are independent of all manufacturers and advertisers, and though they touch only a tiny fraction of the buying public in their circulation, they are increasingly quoted by the popular papers. No doubt the purchase by *Which?* or *Consumer Reports* of the odd faulty product of a small manufacturer, or a biased report, could spell catastrophe. The more power such a magazine has, the more its integrity must be guarded and guaranteed. But it certainly seems to be a useful step in the direction of a more informed and sophisticated buying public, which is the ultimate safeguard against abuses in advertising and promotion.

The marketplace is a hard school, not least for a Christian. But it is wrong to lift up our skirts and withdraw to the cloister. In other generations, Christians have engaged in trade and, by refusing the prevailing customs and setting their own instead, have produced a level of trust between people in their commercial dealings that was not there before. It is in the creation of a positive trust between people that Christians have made their greatest contribution. The destruction of trust is the real loss caused by bribery and unfair and harsh trading. It is only if enough people are honest and fair that trade can grow, and prosperity with it. This should be a proper objective for Christians of our own generation.

10 Making Money in the Stock Market

Ask the average person whether there is a difference between a flier on the stock market and a flier on the horses, and he will probably say there is not. Ask the average stockbroker whether a stock exchange performs a useful social function, and he will almost certainly say it does. Which is right: one, both, or neither?

Most Christians will agree that institutions, financial or otherwise, should have a useful social function. Most Christians would probably also agree that a useful social function should not be carried out in a way that has antisocial consequences, directly or indirectly.

There can be little doubt that in a market economy, the stock exchange fulfills a necessary function. The underlying purpose of all financial institutions is to put savings to the most productive use. Cash in the pocket or in the stocking has an immediate claim on consumption. As soon as this cash is put into a financial institution, the individual waives some part of his immediate claim on it, and it becomes available in one way or another for productive investment.

The terms on which cash goes into the financial institution determine the extent to which it can be committed to productive investment and the extent, on the other hand, of the lender's continuing claim on it. Deposits in banks, for instance, are available on demand, so bank overdrafts are called on demand. Time deposits are callable at a week's notice, giving a little more freedom to the bank in their lending. The skilled banker makes certain that the calls made on him can be matched by the calls he in turn is able to make on those who borrow from him. A banker can lend to finance the borrower's liquid assets like stocks and debts, but he cannot use more than a limited amount of this to finance long-term investment in buildings and machines. If he did, he might be caught in a position where he could not raise the quick money to repay calls made on him by depositors.

FUNCTIONS OF A STOCK EXCHANGE

For long-term investment, other terms and institutions are necessary. There are, broadly, two kinds: long-term loans and risk-bearing stock. The first is repaid only at the end of the term, and the second is normally not repayable at any time. Without the supplementary institution of a stock exchange, an investor would lose all access to his capital; there would be a severe limit to the amount of capital people would be prepared to put into long-term investment on these terms. One of the primary functions of a stock exchange is to combine the needs of industry for long-term investment with the desire of the investor to have ready access to his capital should he need it. It does this by providing a day-to-day market for both loans and risk-bearing stock.

The second function of a stock exchange is the assessment of the economic worth of one investment against another. It must assess the management, the likely demand for the product, the availability of existing supplies, and any other factor that should influence the investor in putting his savings into a particular company or lending to a particular government. The professional name for those who specialize in this function is "investment analyst"; as industry becomes more complex and more highly capitalized, the demands on their skill are increasing.

The market in stocks is determined by the interplay of these two functions. When more people want their money back than want to put it in, stock prices tend to go down; and when there are more investors, prices tend to go up. But when the market is in balance, you can almost always get your money back without loss. Even if it is not quite in balance, the decline in prices tends to attract buyers just as an increase attracts sellers, and this prevents the stocks from becoming too expensive for the new investor to buy.

When investors judge that a company has good management or an exceptional demand for its products, the market tends to mark the price up relative to its current earnings. Instead of showing a dividend yield of 6 percent, it may show one of 3 percent, and this will make a share that was worth $1 now worth $2 in the market. But if a company is judged to have poor management or to be in an industry where capacity outstrips demand, the price will tend to go down relative to earnings.

USEFUL PRICE MOVEMENTS

These price movements are useful to the economy in general. When a price is marked up, it becomes more economical for a company to raise new capital, and when it is marked down, it becomes more difficult. The incoming funds are thus set off in the direction of companies with better management and a higher demand for their products, and are discouraged from moving in the direction of companies with poor management. The market can, of course, be wrong, but it represents the cumulative judgment of thousands of people—judgments that the people are prepared to back with their savings.

The mechanism of the capital market is not ideal. It tends to take, perhaps, rather too short-term a view, and it still tends to be taken in by the glamor of a particular industry or country at a particular time. But this only reflects the moods of human nature and a lack of information. There is little doubt that the market performs a service of considerable magnitude and that it is run, by and large, by able and honorable men. Why is it, then, that a stock exchange is regarded with such suspicion and even hostility by many people?

First of all, there is a sense in which the money market is amoral. Its integrity in dealing with other people's money is beyond question. But it is not set up to be a judge of the social consequences of investment. If there is a demand for cigarettes and beer, it will steer the money very efficiently in the direction of tobacco and breweries. If there is a demand for ice cream, the market will supply the money to make it, regardless of the numbers of people in the country still living in the slums. If a takeover bidder "offers to purchase," the market will not normally ask how he is going to look after long-service employees. Price is the deciding factor. All this can be made to look—and in fact can be—very callous and selfish.

A stockbroker would almost certainly reply that moral judgments are not his function. His clients make the moral judgments and he acts on their instructions. If he did not, they would go elsewhere. If overriding social considerations enter in, then that is up to the government: they are the judges as to what is antisocial and what should be made illegal. Brokers can no more refuse to deal in a company's stocks than the railways, as common carriers can refuse to carry their merchandise.

There is a good deal of integrity in this argument. A stock exchange is not set up to deliver moral judgments. If there appeared to be a demand for a product and the stock exchange became stuffy and refused to deal in the stocks of the manufacturers or distributors, there would very soon be an outcry, and people would ask who they think they are to set themselves up as authorities in such matters. But this is not the whole answer.

Although the stock market as a whole probably should not refuse to deal in the shares of an industry of doubtful social value, there is nothing to compel an individual broker to deal in them. If his clients insist, he can always send them elsewhere (which the railways, as common carriers, cannot do). If a good many brokers acted in this way, the market in the shares would become narrower, their value relative to their yield would be lower, and the industry would find it marginally more expensive to raise money. The result would be a general dampening effect on the doubtful industry.

There is probably another reason for public distrust of the money market. It is essentially an impersonal mechanism which, nevertheless, affects the lives of employees in a very real way. The worker knows that behind the company director, whom he can see and talk to, is the money market—remote, unknowable, and far more important than the individual stockbroker.

Financial journalists say they are very conscious of the difference between the attitude of industry and Wall Street, or its British counterpart, "the City." Both may see the economic necessity of rationalization, but the burden of the human problem weighs more heavily on one than on the other. A former Economic Editor of *The Financial Times* has commented on the rather narrow life of the City. Recruited from the same sort of school, coming up in the same daily train from the same sort of rural retreat, and lunching in the same clubs, they seldom have the opportunity of seeing industrial life at first hand, and their outlook on social problems tends to be a little naïve, though some of the best brokerage firms do visit clients' plants.

The Christian who works on Wall Street will be bound to follow the same pattern of life to some extent, but no one should be able to say of any Christian that he is ill-informed about the way of life of his fellows or that he is careless of the consequences which his actions will have on them. He should almost certainly take some positive action to put this right. He should, perhaps, take the trouble to understand and mix with people in different types of jobs, to visit his clients' plants and listen to the views of those who work there. He might even answer questions from the shop stewards on what Wall Street does for a living!

THE MORALITY OF THE INVESTOR

Behind the stockbroker and the issuing house is the investor, and although the former can plead that they are only part of the mechanism, the latter cannot. He is responsible for the morality as well as the mechanics of every transaction he makes. Investment is in general of high social value. It is by saving and investing instead of spending that we can raise living standards in our own country and elsewhere. Investment provides jobs and makes work less back-breaking. The higher the volume of investment money coming on the market, the lower the rate of interest and the greater the number of investment projects that become economically viable. But a Christian should be more concerned than most with the social direction of investment. He should operate with clear ground rules.

The Church Commissioners of the Church of England are said not to invest in drink, tobacco, or entertainment. Even though a Christian may drink, smoke, or spend on entertainment himself, it is generally felt that it is undesirable for a Christian to make money out of products or activities that do damage to the weaker members of the community. It may be one thing to feel that there is no harm in having a glass of sherry, but another to feel that the more people drink, the richer you will be. For those who feel that social conditions require total abstinence, there is, of course, no question. On the other hand, it seems legalistic to refuse to buy a share in a building company because it may put up an occasional tavern, or in a chain of stores because it may make a fraction of its profits from the sale of tobacco.

There is no major activity that one could feel certain is absolutely free from the taint of evil. If we should not buy shares of a company with a fractional activity of which we disapprove, presumably, by the same token, we should not buy its normal products either. It is hard to believe that a Christian is put upon inquiry to this extent. It is scarcely right to spend our time and energy in straining at gnats even if we do not swallow the camel. What matters is the main activity of the company, the one on which its economics really depend.

A Christian should be concerned for more than money. Directors are ultimately answerable to stockholders for all their policies, but if stockholders are interested in nothing but dividends, it requires a strong sense of duty on the part of the directors to be interested in the social effects of their policies, particularly in areas where there are not legal sanctions to compel their interest. In practice, stockholder control is no longer effective, and there is a strong argument for responsible bodies to identify the social interest and agree with companies the ways in which it can be safeguarded. But even this would not relieve the stockholder of his obligations, and until there is some such body, he has the more obligation to do what he can; and there is in fact much that he can still do.

If, for instance, all stockholders showed a preference for companies whose labor and staff relations were known to be good and avoided those where they were notoriously bad, this would become a factor in the calculations of the capital market and would make life even more difficult for those boards who were careless of industrial relations. If, too, stockholders took the trouble to turn up at annual meetings and asked questions, not only about financial policy, but also about personnel policy, this could do nothing but good. Boards are fairly sensitive to reasoned and sensible criticism at their public meetings, and those who took the trouble would have an influence out of all proportion to their number.

For all these reasons, a long-term investment in a company seems better than an "in-and-out" investment policy. It enables the stockholder to know something of the company in which he has a stake and to feel and exercise a greater responsibility toward it. Perhaps today stockholders sell out a little too easily when things go wrong. Only when they find themselves unexpectedly "locked in" to the investment do they begin to make a fuss. Stocks and shares are commodities, to be bought and sold as shrewdly as other commodities such as sugar, coffee, and tin. But they are more than that. They carry the legal control of companies employing thousands of citizens, and to that extent they must be handled more responsibly. Long-term investment is more than the stockbrokers' "Put them away and forget about them."

INVESTING CHURCH FUNDS

In investing church funds, a church may not wish to have its name associated with particular political views, but this should not prevent it from taking a responsible view as a stockholder in matters where the stockholders can and should exercise moral judgments. Indeed, not to act when it has the power to act is in itself a decision to back the policies of the directors. If their moral judgment is considered wrong, the church will not have avoided criticism by its inaction.

The Christian who takes a responsible view of shareholding will want his investment to be under his own direct control as far as practicable. For this reason he will probably prefer to hold shares in his own name. This point applies particularly to funds invested in the name of a church or Christian charity. For instance, if a church bought shares in an investment trust, this would probably have some drink, tobacco, and entertainment shares in the portfolio, and this would be known by anyone who cared to look at the stock registers and the portfolio of the trust. This was the case in the United States in the late sixties when, having made public pronouncements opposing the U.S. role in the Vietnam war, church officials in some mainline denominations found, to their embarrassment, that their church investment portfolios included industries producing materiel such as napalm that they had specifically condemned.

The lesson of such situations is that the church may well be blamed even if the final use of its assets is out of its control. In a noteworthy British incident, at Paddington Estates, it was discovered that some church property had been sublet for wrongful use; even though the church had no control over the subletting and reaped no financial benefit, what stuck in the public's mind was that it was church-owned property.

However, it would be a harsh rule that excluded the individual Christian from investing in unit trusts, particularly if he were the sort of small investor for whom the trusts were designed. For this kind of investor, direct investment is not really practicable, nor would he exercise the same influence at company meetings as investors with a more typical size of holding. It would be hard too to condemn such trusts for the small investor without also condemning life insurance and pension schemes, and since these are the chief forms of saving, we would need to be on sure ground before doing so. If a majority of their revenue normally came from doubtful investments, this would be grounds for objection. But these investments are normally a negligible portion of any portfolio and would not normally make any difference to the investor's dividend or to the size of the pension.

Nevertheless, a Christian who has sufficient capital and can, with advice, make direct investments should take a positive view of the use of his money. He cannot only keep clear of doubtful investments, but also see that his money does useful work. He might, for instance, think that instead of investing in banking or finance-company stocks at home, he should invest in a bank that helps to finance programs for development in the newly developing countries.

Although most Christians who want to be responsible investors will put their money in for the long term, the "in-and-out" investor does have a very useful function. Without a body of investors prepared to buy on a falling market and to sell on a rising one, the market would be much more unstable, and the small investor who wanted his money out in a hurry would be in a greater risk of selling at a loss. But this is a highly specialized function and not an activity for everyone. It requires ample funds, a highly specialized knowledge, and a steady nerve. In London this function is partly performed by the stock-jobbers, and in New York by the specialists, both of whom buy and sell on their own account in a fairly narrow section of the market. Their buying and selling absorbs the first shock of a general movement in their market. They are well-informed about the stocks in which they specialize and sensitive to any news or moods that will affect their market. Beyond the specialists and jobbers are private investors, who may not operate on a day-to-day basis but who, nevertheless, have the resources and experience to take a short-term position in the market. Their activities should also, at least in theory, provide a steadying influence.

THE MAN IN THE STREET

But it by no means follows that what is right for the specialist is right for the man in the street. Where the specialists take a carefully calculated risk, the man in the street may be doing no more than taking a flier. There is, of course, a degree of risk in every investment we make—when we buy a car or a house or educate our children. But we try in all these cases to minimize the risk. We do not run the risk for the fun of the thing, which is the essence of gambling.

There are two ways of looking at this, first in relation to the economic function and second in relation to the right use of our own money. Gauging the right price for a particular share at a particular time is a highly complex matter. To take a view that a share is under- or over-priced at a given moment, and will shortly go up or down, requires considerable skill and judgment. Insofar as the judgment is right, it will avoid the share becoming too expensive or too cheap, will swing the share back into line, and do the market a service. Insofar as the judgment is wrong, it will swing the share price the wrong way and do the market a disservice. Too often the ignorant amateur plunges off in the wrong direction, led on by mood, hearsay, and half-truth, and the market goes to giddy heights or plunges to the depths. This does no good to anyone, least of all to the amateur himself, who usually gets his fingers burned. Our first question, when tempted to buy with a view to a quick sale, is whether we really know what we are up to. If not, we can hardly pretend to have any useful economic function.

There is all the difference in the world between normal business risk and speculation. For instance, a property company may have a large tract of land that amounts to say 10 percent of its assets. The land may be without services and even without proper zoning for development. It may still have heavy development risks. It may be heavily mortgaged. In these circumstances, the property company may feel it prudent to spread the risk by selling part of the equity, making the dangers quite plain for all to see. Its own stake comes down to 5 percent or even 2 percent of its total investment. This may diminish its potential profits, but it is wise spreading of the risk. Too often, however, some people take up the shares in quite a different mood. There is a fashion for property stocks or a rush of popularity for the area and wild dreams of capital gains, all of which sweep aside the cautious statements of the property company. The frantic buying and selling of the shares bears no relation to the plain facts of life. A whole lot of people burn their fingers. A small number of operators skilled in this sort of situation make quite a lot of money, there is a violent reaction, that kind of stock drops out of favor, funds for housing development dry up, and five years later a young couple pay a good deal more for a place to live than they need have done. But for the distortion of the market through greed, this need never have happened.

There are legitimate risks that bring capital gains. Someone may buy a large block of shares in a company when they are at a low price, because he knows and has confidence in the management. He may, by sustaining the share price, help to keep them in the saddle over a rough spell and enable them to carry out a beneficial long-term program. His capital gain at the end is the reward for intelligent risk, and he has achieved a socially beneficial purpose.

It seems possible to make a lot of money in the stock market by doing very little, and this possibility is open to those who are already rich. Part of the answer to this is that it is also possible to lose a lot of money. Another part is that it is not only stock exchange values that rise with inflation. Values of houses rise too. But if the institution does perform a useful social function, it is better to adjust personal incomes by taxation than to take the considerable risks involved in altering the mechanics of the institution itself.

Even if we do have some knowledge, we need to be careful to keep our activities porportionate to our resources. It is one thing to put 10 percent of our resources into a speculative position; it is a very different thing to plunge the lot and, even worse, to put in more than we have and borrow the margin. The worst crashes on the stock exchange have had, as a major contributing factor, the forced and frantic sales of those who had been operating on margin and did not have the ready cash to pay. These people were not only gambling their own and other people's money; they were gambling with the stability of the exchange. Part of the argument for a market economy, including the capital market, is that it is a delicate self-correcting mechanism. Speculation puts a strain on this mechanism and can only do it harm. In extreme cases it provokes boom and slump, brings the market economy itself into disrepute, and encourages people to turn in disillusion to more arbitrary ways of managing economic affairs. Many forces combined to bring Hitler to power in Germany in 1933, but not least were the economic disasters in the years just before.

The stock market is not for gambling, but it is possible to use it to gamble. It is there for a serious and constructive purpose, and it is possible by misusing it to frustrate its purpose. In practice this means that most of us, if we want to invest, should do so on a long-term basis and after taking skilled and experienced advice. Only if we have the capital, experience, and skill of a specialist, and can make a positive contribution to the stability and liquidity of the market, should we go into the business of short-term buying and selling of stocks. It goes without saying that a Christian should not be led astray by the sin of covetousness. He should not come to the business of investing in a greedy frame of mind, and in avoiding these temptations he will no doubt save himself and others a good deal of trouble. The man who is greedy will try to get out far more than he puts in. He wants more than the rate of interest and the risk premium, and in order to get it he usually has to cut a few corners. If he loses his own money, that is no more than he deserves; but very often he will have involved others in his disasters.

A FOUNDATION OF TRUST

Whatever their faults, the institutions of the City (the Stock Exchange, Lloyds, the deposit banks, the issuing houses, the discount houses, the commodity exchanges, and insurance companies) and the comparable institutions on Wall Street (stock and commodity exchanges, bank and trust companies, brokerage houses, and insurance companies) are honorable institutions, each with its professional code. This code may not be sufficiently wide to take in all the broad social effects of what they do, but it is sufficient to enable their fellows to trust them with hundreds of millions of dollars of their savings, and rarely is there any abuse of trust. When there is, the City will more often than not come to the rescue to see that the ordinary person is not harmed. This degree of mutual trust and self-discipline is rare in human affairs and makes a contribution to wealth and well-being, as well as to ethical standards, which can only be measured when it is compared with countries that do not have similar standards and institutions. In the United States this self-discipline is supplemented by a body of federal and state securities legislation, and government commissions to enforce it.

In the last of Anthony Trollope's novels, *The Way We Live Now,* the villain is the promoter of shares in an American railroad that is to run across the prairies from north to south. The whole exercise is an economic confidence trick that requires the presence on his board of titled and ignorant people in whom the investing public will have confidence, but who will not ask any awkward questions. The other ingredients are human gullibility—believing what we want to believe—and greed.

In every generation there seems to be a similar rash of gullibility and greed. The author was trained as a chartered accountant by seniors who had been through the boom of the twenties and the crash of 1931. They had investigated the stock promoters of their day who had sold shares to build up paper empires, paying dividends from capital as the stock market rose and being caught short as the crash came and all new shares became unsalable. The methods were the same, though the stock promotion stories were altered to appeal to the public of the twenties. Memories of the thirties faded and no one believed it could happen again, but the late sixties' mergermania and the early seventies' property boom contained just the same stock promotion techniques.

In Britain and America the young whiz-kids of the mergermania were going to take over old and fuddy-duddy business of every kind, smarten the management, and put the assets to work. The price of conglomerate shares soared, and even when an acquisition went sour, the promoters could buy the earnings of a new company to cover up, until finally the whiz-kid management overstretched itself, the losses could not be hidden, and the conglomerate stock dropped in price and became unsalable.

The British property boom was similar. As industrial trouble mounted and industrial shares failed to hold their value, the property promoters' line was that bricks and mortar would not lose their value and that rents would always rise faster than the cost of running an office block or shopping center. They raised enormous mortgages, which were to be repaid out of sales valuations, and those in turn were based on continuously rising rentals. For two or three years it looked and behaved as if they had at last discovered the philosopher's stone. The author happened to be chief executive at this time of a contracting company with a long-established property holding and development business, and he felt at firsthand the full pressures of this extraordinary boom, which was financed through mushroom "secondary" banks by large and reputable financial institutions that should have known better. At the end of 1973, the boom—inevitably—boiled over, property companies went bankrupt, and the secondary banks would have followed them, bringing down other more reputable financial institutions, if the Bank of England had not been authorized to lend them enough money to keep afloat under new management.

At the height of the South Sea bubble, the stock boom of the early eighteenth century, Sarah, Duchess of Marlborough, said, "The thing is ridiculous," and sold her entire stock, her sharp common sense saving her and her family and leaving us with a comment that really cannot be bettered. But for every duchess who is able to get out at the top, there are thousands of small investors who lose more money than they can possibly afford and millions of workers who come to believe that the stock exchange is no more than a lottery at best and a swindle at worst. Those who had to talk to meetings of workers in the boom know how much the free-market economy was identified with the stock and property promotions. And the politicians who think a free market is the best way to promote the nation's wealth feel that their whole position has been undermined. The British Prime Minister Edward Heath said that he had given British business their freedom and all he got back was a property boom.

The lesson a Christian draws is that the handling of money needs the utmost honesty and integrity and that the system under which financial institutions operate must promote these qualities and must discourage the opposite by regulation, supervision, and sanctions. At each stock-promotion boom, the regulations are tightened and more loopholes are closed.

In Britain so far, it has been considered enough to rely in the main on voluntary self-discipline by financial institutions under the eye of the Governor of the Bank of England. The United States has made more formal regulations by the Securities and Exchange Commission, and Britain has been moving slowly in that direction. Maybe the time has come to move faster. Meanwhile, an ordinary Christian who handles the money of others should do what he can to set the highest standards of trust.

11 The Christian as an Employer

IN LARGE FIRMS the proportion of active Christians on the board of directors will be small. Therefore, in the strict sense, a large firm will not be a Christian employer in the way that a small family business, run and dominated by a Christian, could be said to be a Christian firm. Even though a Christian manager or director in a large business will normally be in a minority, there ought, nevertheless, to be a standard that he can set or put into practice as far as circumstances allow. A Christian recognizes that society will never be perfect; even the most Christian firm will have its faults. But this does not make a Christian despair of bringing about a *more* Christian order in society and in industry. If we can get some improvement because we have raised a Christian voice, that is far better than washing our hands of the whole thing.

There will also, of course, be a minimum standard. If his colleagues fall below this, a Christian would feel bound to dissociate himself from them, either by registering a contrary vote or by resignation. It is difficult to generalize on cases where a Christian would feel that he could not serve on the board of a company. If he is already a member of the board, he should not normally resign simply because he finds himself overruled by a majority on a matter of technical judgment. Even on a moral matter where a board had tried to exercise responsible judgment and the decision had gone the other way, he would not automatically be right to resign.

There are, however, cases where a Christian conscience will diverge from those of others. For instance, if a decision involves the personal interest of some of the board and is acknowledged to be damaging to the company's interests, but the majority, nevertheless, are not prepared to jeopardize their own individual positions by active opposition, a Christian can hardly go along with them. This sort of situation could arise when, for instance, a minority want to have friends and relatives appointed to key positions that are beyond their capabilities; or where the siting of new plants is governed by personal whims and not by the economics of labor supply or distribution; or where there is investment of the company's money in marginal projects because of pressure of outside friendship. It might be wrong to resign for an isolated case, but right if a clear trend had developed and could not be checked.

AN IMAGE OF RESPECTABILITY

There is no doubt that many graduates choose professions rather than business because they feel that the professions have clear-cut codes of conduct enforceable by well-designed sanction and that, for these reasons, professions have a higher standard than business. One senior director of a large and reputable company still gives his occupation as "engineer" rather than company director because, he says, it sounds more respectable. Even where graduates do "go into business," there is a preference for managerial positions in very large companies that have some reputation for their ethical standards as over against board positions on small public or private companies. This is not, therefore, an imaginary problem.

It is not enough to say that no one today expects a junior executive director to take his legal responsibilities to the stockholders too much to heart. This may be true, but directors cannot be satisfied with the public's attitude toward companies resulting from this situation. The British Institute of Directors has taken this seriously and has done some work on codes and boardroom practice, and it seems that more needs to be done. In the meantime, those who are offered board appointments ought to take a long, hard look at the situation before they become involved, and they should make quite certain that the standards of the board are the sort they can live with. When issues arise with which they disagree, they should put their views courteously, but they should not allow themselves to be intimidated.

While most decisions are in fact basically technical, there is probably a tendency in industrial society to regard *all* decisions as technical. There is a regrettable tendency to treat erratic behavior in humans like the erratic behavior of machines, and to wish that human beings could be made to react with the same precision. This results, when it happens, in an impression of bleak, impersonal, or machine-like efficiency coupled with a lack of human warmth. A Christian should be sensitive to personal and moral issues and should see the moral issue when there is one and when his colleagues may see only the technical.

The author has been around scores of shop floors both in the companies he has served and in others. In Export Year alone he visited about fifty plants, large and small. In all these plants it was possible to tell almost at once whether personal relations were good or bad. In the plants with poor relations, the management talked about the machinery and ignored the people. In those with good relations the people were introduced by name, with some account of what they did—even at times their hobbies: "Jim is a champion angler; he fishes with shore-lines." The author will not forget visiting a factory with a friendly, warm-hearted cabinet minister who insisted on talking to everyone, while perspiration rolled down the face of the embarrassed factory manager who knew no one. At the next factory, the owner introduced every apprentice personally and with great pride. The first factory had a prolonged and bitter strike shortly afterward. The chairman of a big car manufacturer told the author that he went to all the company's main social events so that he could meet the majority of the workers and their wives for a friendly chat. In his time the company never had a strike. His successor was a hard-liner whose watchword was "Management must manage." He did not last long, but long enough to destroy the trust his predecessor had built.

Treating employees like human beings is not just a matter of glad-handing or of memorizing names and hobbies. It means really listening to what they are saying, treating it with respect, and doing whatever can be done about it. It means seeing things from their point of view and trying to relate whatever else is happening to that point of view. The slogan of Export Year was not "Export or die," which is just not credible; or "Exporting is fun," which it isn't; or "Export for your country," which is too remote; or "Exporting is profitable," which it may be; but "Exports equals jobs," which said that if the company succeeds in building export markets, it makes existing jobs more secure and creates new ones. It was a slogan which met the workers' need and with which they could identify. All this friendliness did not stop a union official from arriving at a meeting to say, "All I want to know is how much more and when." But it did mean that those on the union side kicked him under the table and told him to be quiet.

A Christian, as well as having a general desire for justice, has also the particular command of Paul to treat all his workers justly and fairly. Anyone who has ever tried to work out a "just wage" will know how insuperable the difficulties appear, but a Christian must at least make the effort. Justice should take into account the different kinds of skills, work, risk, responsibility, and enjoyment in the different jobs. Absolute justice is impossible, because absolute measurement of the differing degrees of these factors is not possible. However, certain broad standards can be applied. In order to avoid the evils of sweated labor, there should be a minimum wage that will give a reasonable basic standard of living. The payment of the minimum should not be waived even if the employer cannot pay. No one should be allowed to take people into his employment unless he is able to pay them.

There should be differentials for greater responsibility and for jobs that require years of specialized training. Differentials are, however, a difficult problem, and it is not possible to lay down exact standards for them. But it is often possible to see anomalies, and glaring anomalies should always be put right. It is hard to justify payment to the hospital porter of a larger salary than that paid to the doctor who is a resident surgeon. The wider the field, the harder it is to regulate the differentials. But in a smaller field like a particular plant or company, the application of a differential is a reasonably practicable proportion.

DIFFERENTIALS FOR SKILLS

Even with its disadvantages, free bargaining is probably as good a solution as any other for settling wage rates. But differentials are fair only if there is freedom of opportunity to enter into the skilled trades and professions that claim the differentials. No trade or profession should create an artificial shortage to give its members a better bargaining position.

Although the law of supply and demand avoids the shortages that would be caused by a rigid wage structure, there should be some sort of relationship between the level of a man's remuneration and the value of his service to society. In Britain, the older professions, which demand a high degree of minimum skill because of their importance to society, oblige their members to charge a minimum scale that is high enough to reflect their value to society. The forces of supply and demand are not allowed to affect this minimum. No architect can try to create a demand for his services by cutting his fees. In the United States, some groups of professionals publish average or "reasonable" fee schedules, but the establishment of a rigid minimum is illegal.

This principle of a minimum differential for skill could probably be applied more widely and would ensure that where the public required and relied on skill, that skill was forthcoming. This might happen, perhaps, only with a considerable time lag when demand was rising, since the training periods of these professionals is very long.

Although the Christian has a duty to love his neighbor, this is not irreconcilable with the duty as a manager to exercise discipline. Discipline is necessary in all human organizations, the more so in organizations where people's livelihood and, indeed, their safety depend on everyone's keeping to the rules. If one member of a group endangers the safety or livelihood of others, then justice demands that he be subject to discipline. If this rule of law is not observed, if actions become arbitrary and irrational, the whole group is damaged. A Christian has a duty not only to love, but also to be just. Love without justice is sentimentality. A Christian's duty of love is not only to the individual who requires discipline, but to all employees and others who may be affected by the conduct of that individual. The more human beings have to work together, the more they need to subject themselves to discipline. The less they subject themselves to discipline, the less effective their common organization will be. Discipline in the workplace should not be arbitrary. Punishments should fit the offenses committed, and provisions should be made for employees to be heard in their own defense, and to appeal any serious punishments.

Employees are dismissed as a matter of discipline when they have not done their job properly, but also, more frequently, when there ceases to be a job for them to do. There are certain industries where it is difficult to offer regular employment, and dismissing the labor force at the end of the job is an inherent part of the contract of engagement. But casual labor is not normally a desirable state of affairs; most people feel the need of a greater security than is given by engagement on a day-to-day basis. In industries where labor is casual, there are ways of minimizing the casual nature of the labor, or of rearranging or reorganizing the industry by agreement so that people are protected against sudden changes in fortune. Where an industry normally offers regular employment, a Christian will want to be foremost in minimizing the effect of permanent layoffs where these are economically necessary. Christians should also support government policies which provide for local or national layoff agreements, since these are aimed to protect the dignity of the worker and avoid treatment of him as a piece of redundant machinery.

If it is right for workers to combine to negotiate with employers, it can hardly be wrong for employers to combine in trade federations in order to conduct negotiations with employees on behalf of whole industries. The advantage is that all competitors in the same industry have to pay the same wage, and this makes the negotiations of any increases a good deal easier for the union. On the other hand, while federations have proved to be a convenient method of bargaining, in times of full employment they have been the means of passing on wage increases to the customer and in time of unemployment they might be the means of weighting the bargaining power unduly against the worker. If there is nothing intrinsically wrong with federations, this does not mean that they are ideal or that everything they do is necessarily right.

The rules of union negotiations are not substantially different from the rules of any other negotiation. Each side should keep to high standards in their advocacy, and there is no obligation on either side to disclose its full hand. However, the more the employer is willing to trust the trustworthy unionist with information, the better the relationship ought to be. Both parties would rightly expect the other to look after their respective interests.

SHARING IN PROFITABILITY

There are three main claimants on the improvements in profitability made by an individual company: the customer, the employee, and the stockholder. The good manager will not try to provide for one at the expense of the others. He should try to give a bit more than the average to each of them and provide for it by a higher-than-average standard of managerial competence and hard work.

Threats have often been part of industrial bargaining, and a Christian has to decide on the extent to which they are justified. Even if he thinks they are justified, they should certainly never be empty. An empty threat is a form of deception, and a Christian cannot justify this. Even if the threat can be implemented, a coercive threat should not be made where the act of coercion itself would be wrong. On the other hand, it is not wrong to bring to the notice of the other side courses of action that are open to your own side and that are fair and in good faith. It is also quite legitimate to expose the pretensions of the other side. In dealing with the Pharisees, our Lord Himself did not hesitate to do this. When they demanded the truth on what the basis of His authority was, He demanded in turn the truth on the authority of John the Baptist. They were unwilling to commit themselves to an answer, because any answer had awkward implications, and this made it impossible for them to insist that our Lord give them an answer.

It is quite legitimate to put the other side in a position where they must concede the same standards of truth and information that they themselves are demanding. The quality of truth in a Christian's statement should be uncompromising, and a Christian's reputation should be such that all who deal with him should know that what he says is true and fair. His yes should be yes and his no should be no without the need of emphasis.

Those who are opposed to paternalism in management are bound to take the view that the management cannot be responsible for the morals of its employees outside the time and place of employment, provided their behavior does not interfere with the job itself. The manager's position is a functional one. His only authority over people lies in his function and in their acceptance of it, and where their actions have no relation to his function as a manager, his authority does not apply.

Where the employee's job requires that the holder should command respect locally, where he has to have a certain degree of authority and standing, then his behavior outside business hours is not, however, irrelevant to his job. If his behavior becomes so notorious as to undermine the respect necessary for his job, his employer has to take this into account. In many cases in practice, where someone has made a mess of his private life, he will want to put things right; very often the employer can rescue the situation with some legal aid or with personal advice. This is a very delicate matter, and more harm than good can be done by an overzealous manager, even if he interferes with the best possible motives. A Christian should aim to be the sort of person who inspires a high standard of behavior, but he should combine this with a sympathetic nature so that those who get in a mess can come to him more easily. While a Christian has no right to impose his standards on the private lives of his employees, he may find ways of helping without interfering with their essential freedom.

On the job, a Christian will want to keep as high a moral standard as he can. Christian doctrine makes it perfectly clear that there are certain rules of conduct in our relations to each other which help those relations. The Christian employer, personnel officer, or welfare officer will try to see, as far as possible, that within the factory gates those roles are kept and that employees while on duty are sober, moral, and responsible in their behavior toward each other.

PRESENTING A CHRISTIAN WITNESS

Many Christian employers with small businesses, where they know all their work people, have taken the view that they have a responsibility to present the Christian faith to those who work for them. Only those who have a firm Christian faith can realize the desperate anxiety someone can have for his fellows who are not Christians. But direct evangelization by management can lead to the most unpleasant forms of hypocrisy. Some businessmen, realizing this, try to remain behind the scenes themselves and bring in an evangelist from outside.

However anxious a Christian may be for those who work for him, the company—apart possibly from the small, private, family company—is not the enlargement of one man's household. This is a patriarchal concept and is normally quite inapplicable to today's relationship of stockholders, directors, and employees.

It is right that people should know that we are Christians. It is also likely, since people may be associated in companies over long periods of time and since most facets of an executive's character are the subject of comment, that a great many people will have the opportunity of judging the effects of the Christian faith on his behavior. It should not be necessary to import evangelists or chaplains in order to bear a Christian witness. If executives do bring in speakers or chaplains, this should be in addition to their own personal witness. It is, in any case, quite impracticable to think they can avoid responsibility or in any way remain behind the scenes. They would be held directly responsible for subjecting their work people to their own particular philosophy of life. If an evangelical Christian does this, he cannot object to it being done by Catholics, Moonies, atheists, or Jehovah's Witnesses in the businesses where they are the employers.

The Bible makes it quite clear that the churches themselves are major instruments for the propagation of the Christian faith. If a Christian businessman wants to see that Christian teaching is available to employees, his first responsibility should be to support the local churches in which there is good Christian teaching. If there is no suitable local church, he might establish a chaplaincy, but it should not be too closely associated with the job, and attendance should be voluntary in fact as well as in name.

Some Christians have written pamphlets explaining the reason for their faith and have distributed them to employees. These have done good without forcing an employee to react publicly to the message or embarrassing him if he does not want to listen. It goes without saying that whatever funds are required for this should be privately subscribed. Christians must bear in mind that it imposes a most unfair strain in a mixed society if the boss is strongly identified with one particular group of his employees.

Where a chaplaincy has been created, if it is to be on the premises, the request for it should come from the church or the employees themselves or both. To avoid abuse, it should be quite independent of the management and should not take advantage of a privileged position to proselytize those of other religious groups. The Christian would be unnatural if he did not want others to hear the Christian gospel, but he should have faith in the innate power of a Christian life and of the truth of the message to make their marks. There should be no need to override sound social relationships or engage in petty maneuvering in order to get a hearing for the Christian faith. Where people are reluctant to listen, we should look first not at the mechanics of propaganda but at ourselves.

If some Christian employees want to have meetings on the premises, then the meetings should be open. If they do not want to have them openly, they should have them in their homes because, while nothing in a free society should ever stop like-minded people from meeting together in private, it is most undesirable that there should be a "secret society" in any way associated with the employing company.

An employer should not put himself in the position where the workers feel that he regards religion as something that will keep them quiet and well-behaved. There are those who will be only too quick to see that religion is the "opium of the people." What matters more than anything else is that the employer shall be regarded as fair and will be seen to have the interests of his workers at heart. There are a thousand and one ways in which he can show his Christianity in action, and in which he can be known to do what he does because he is a Christian.

12 The Organization

However important the broad, general principles of Christianity in industrial affairs, the problems confronting most Christians most often are those that face them as Christians within a secular organization. These problems all vary greatly, but their one common thread is the conflict between the unyielding standards by which the Christian considers himself bound and the demands made on him by the organization in which he works—demands which cannot be expected, since it employs Christians and non-Christians alike, to conform to every Christian ideal.

One obvious problem arises from the nature of secular organization. If all people are equal, is it right to have a hierarchical organization at all? Is its authority legitimate? Are its trappings a farce in which a Christian should have no part?

It is likely that far more resentment is caused by visible differences between people at their place of work than by the differences in the amount of money paid to them at the end of the week or month. A Christian is bound to question whether the hierarchical structure of business that causes these differentials and this resentment is justified, but all experience of human affairs shows that it seems to be a necessary way of organizing large-scale enterprise among fallible human beings. All other large-scale organizations seem to require their hierarchy. It is true in national and local government. It is true of the army. It is true of the law. In Britain, a judge at the assizes is bound to stay in his lodging and eat with his peers. He is not allowed to accept hospitality in the neighborhood. It is his job to sit in judgment on his fellows, and this function requires that he be a certain distance from them. This is an extreme case, but in a lesser way and in a more limited sphere, the manager must give his judgment in matters affecting the lives of those who work under him; his function, therefore, requires a certain degree of authority and dignity. The hierarchy of authority is a functional necessity, both for the forming of decisions and for their execution.

Christians will, however, try to see that distinctions of rank are the absolute minimum necessary for the function. While familiarity can breed contempt, a Christian will do his best to see that he is respected for his qualities and not for his trappings. Certainly a Christian employer will try to avoid building the kind of organization that appears to need ten different grades of dining room to preserve the subtle distinction between rank and rank. If we can make top-grade dining rooms available to anyone for an extra payment, so much the better.

Where there is no question of authority, the hierarchy is probably not necessary. It does not seem necessary, for instance, where a job may require a high degree of personal skill but makes no demands whatever on a man's character. It is also probably true that the more primitive the society, the greater the requirement for outward and visible trappings of authority. The more sophisticated and educated the society, the more authority will be understood and accepted without the need for visible pomp and show. In these circumstances, not only is too much pomp and show unnecessary, it can also be an insult to the intelligence.

A Christian should realize, more than the next man, that whatever ability and intelligence he has and whatever qualities of authority he may possess, they are not of his own making. They were given to him by his Creator. This should make him humble. He should also, if he obeys Paul's command to examine himself and James's command to confess his faults, be more aware than most of his own shortcomings and this too ought to make him humble. This should counterbalance in a Christian the temptation to arrogance and should make him a more pleasant person to live with and to work for.

OUTWARD CHRISTIAN OBSERVANCES

Another set of problems arises if and when the few outward Christian observances conflict with the apparent necessities of the job. The Christian faith puts more emphasis on our attitude of mind and our behavior toward God and our fellows than on outward ceremony, but there are, nevertheless, a limited number of observances that are almost entirely confined to Christians. Perhaps the most important of these is the observance of Sunday as a holy day.

Although the Jews had, under their ceremonial law, many observances that are not binding on Christians, the observance of one day in seven as a holy day dedicated to God cannot be avoided on the grounds that it is simply a relic of Jewish ceremony. It is part of the moral law and is introduced as early as the second and third chapters of Genesis. It has been enshrined in the Ten Commandments, which embody the moral law and are binding on all. The method of observance of one day in seven may be open, but the obligation to observe it is absolute. What our Lord makes clear in the New Testament is that the Christian's observance of one day in seven is not to be mechanical, and it should certainly not cause suffering to his fellows. From this we can deduce that medical and other public services must be carried on. Once a way of life has been geared to these services, they cannot be turned off twenty-four hours in each week without physical hardship.

Today it is not only public services that continue to work on Sunday. In highly capitalized industry—particularly process industry—it is necessary in greater or lesser degree to keep a plant going around the clock seven days a week. As the law stands, no single competing company could step out of line, even if it were physically possible. The law on the one hand permits Sunday working and, on the other, enforces competition. It is quite possible, therefore, for a Christian engineer or chemist to find that Sunday work at fairly regular intervals is an inescapable part of his profession. A Christian will want to keep Sunday work to a minimum and to support legislation limiting work on Sunday. If he is in business on his own, he should certainly limit his work on Sunday even if it means making less profit. In the old days, Welsh farmers never used a sunny Sunday to bring in the harvest, and many Christian farmers stick to the same rule today. But a Christian employer who has a great number of employees to think of will not want to risk their jobs; if the industrial process requires seven days' working and if failure to do this would as the law now stands put him out of business, then he should not put his employees' jobs at risk. If the essence of a business is weekend trade, then a Christian is better out of it. "The sabbath was made for man, and not man for the sabbath" (Mark 2:27), but a Christian will want to observe one day as God's day and will make every endeavor to do so.

A further set of problems arises when a Christian's social life with one set of standards meets the social life of the organization that may have a quite different set of standards. When he is at work, a Christian has a functional occupation that he can and should do whole-heartedly. When he is at home, he can set his own standards of behavior. There is, however, a point at which he meets the people with whom he works on a social basis, and for many this takes the form of office parties. If he is an employer, this is an obligation he cannot and should not escape; but even if his job does not demand it, he will think twice before he opts out of all social activity.

MORAL STANDARDS

Alcoholism is an increasing problem in industry. It is quite clear from the teaching of the Bible that in itself drink is not wrong. It is equally clear that excessive drinking *is* wrong. Until about a hundred years ago, alcoholic drink was probably a necessity of life, but the last hundred years has produced many alternatives, including pure water. In that time many Christians have felt that complete personal abstinence might well help to raise the moral standards. A Christian who takes this line should not appear to be censorious or legalistic. If he has decided that he personally should not drink, he can hold firmly and unself-consciously to his orange juice. In matters where there is no clear-cut commandment of right or wrong, a Christian must be an example and not a cause of offense. A great many people who are not Christians refuse to drink and hold to their positions firmly and cheerfully without offense. This is not a position, therefore, that a Christian needs to find awkward or embarrassing. There are enough pressures today to social conformity in drinking to make a positive case for those who are prepared to stand out, if only to help other and weaker nonconformists keep face.

If Christians have a fault today, it is not that they are entitled to their views on drinking and gambling, but that they tend to limit worldliness to these things. The scope of worldliness is much larger. A teetotaler who spends his company's money on items of pure prestige can still be guilty of worldliness. The important thing to a Christian is that he should set his standards by his faith and that he should not be put off his stride by the views of the world.

This holds good particularly in a Christian's attitude toward the problems that arise from the competition for promotion which is an almost inevitable part of any large organization. There has always been and will always be competition for office. Outside of business, the rules are fairly well defined, but within the new and large business organizations the proper rules of conduct are not always so clear. There is an essential difference between normal progression up a company ladder and what is colloquially known as "the rat race." What goes on very largely depends on the ground rules or the lack of ground rules laid down by the company. A company can, for instance, exacerbate the competition by pressing, as some do, for 100 percent of the employee's devotion and loyalty. This breeds an introverted and unhealthy atmosphere, and promotion decisions become far more important than they should be. It should not be assumed by the company that it is desirable for everyone to have promotion within the company as the overwhelming ambition of his life. For those who cannot achieve it, this ambition is a treadmill; they should have the option to step off it without ill-feeling.

For those who do not feel that their present job allows them to give of their best, it is perfectly proper to go on until they feel they have hit their ceiling. It is, of course, hard to know when the next job is over your ceiling until you have actually tried it. The person who is prepared to take on responsibility keeps on finding himself somewhat above his theoretical ceiling. But usually, sooner or later, he gets on top of his job. The difficulty too often is to find people who are prepared to accept responsibility. This is true in professions outside industry. Many school teachers, for instance, do not wish to become principals; they much prefer teaching and do not want to take on the administrative chores and the unpopular decisions of a head.

When we consider promotion we have to be very honest with ourselves. There is all the difference in the world between wanting "power over" and being anxious for "service to." Ambition must not become our idol, and we must not resort to methods or strategems in order to achieve it. In competition for jobs it is, of course, right to present our case if we feel that we are liable to misrepresentation by others. On the other hand, we should not always be pressing ourselves forward. In the highly competitive world of advertising, it is considered right to praise your own products, but wrong to "knock" your competitors: this is not a bad rule in competition for jobs. A good boss naturally makes it much easier. Most managers agree that in order to diminish areas of conflict and misunderstanding, it is desirable to have a clear demarcation line between colleagues. In this case it is a culpable abdication of responsibility to blur demarcation lines deliberately in order to see "who will swallow up who," but this kind of attitude is, unfortunately, not unknown.

Even those who, like Sir Winston Churchill, are plainly ambitious have been prepared to put ambition aside for the sake of principle and spend long years in the wilderness. When, in May 1940, office seemed near, Churchill defended his chief in the critical debate rather than join those who wanted to bring him down. Those of us who have minor ambitions would do well to follow his example. There is too much emphasis today on success and too little on conduct and character. Our

Lord is quite clear about this. He commends the man who takes the lower place and moves higher only when others come and fetch him.

This should be our rule, even if there are problems in practice. If an activity associated with our own responsibilities is being mishandled and no proper attention is being paid to it, there is nothing wrong in suggesting that it should be taken under our own wing, particularly if this is necessary in order to do our job effectively. People do not object to overt approaches like this. What they do object to is empire-accumulation where the motive is power and self-aggrandizement, carried out not overtly but by discreet maneuvering. Most people know when it is one and when it is the other.

HAVING INTEGRITY AS A COLLEAGUE

The Christian virtues of a colleague should not only be negative ones. It would probably be agreed that the virtue or value above all others in a colleague is integrity. The main content of integrity is honesty, but there is also an element of consistency. Everyone wants the kind of persons as a colleague with whom you know where you stand, who will not shift his ground under pressure, who will accept responsibility and not try to shuffle it off onto his superiors or colleagues.

The Christian's integrity is of a very practical kind. He should never "pass the buck" when something goes wrong. His loyalty to his colleagues should prevent him from telling stories about them which in any way discredit them. Even though he should be outspoken before a decision has been made, he should respect it, once it is made, whether or not he agreed with it in the first place. The motto on President Truman's desk, "The buck stops here," is an appropriate one for a Christian. The sense of peace which his faith gives him should keep him from moods of black despair that often affect the person who has no faith. His quiet confidence should keep him from being jumpy or nervy and, assuming that this does not come from ignorance or micawberism, he should be cheerful, buoyant, and resilient in difficult situations.

Above all, a Christian should try to give practical help to others in their careers. He should never be one to hoard his expertise in order to make himself indispensable. Everyone, looking back over his own professional career, has cause to be grateful to someone who has taken time and trouble to give him, through personal instruction, the kind of things that can never be found out just through reading books. A Christian's love for others should cause those who work with him remember him as someone who has been generous with his own experience.

Some Christians are unsure of the extent to which they should feel free to use their place of work as an active field for evangelism. It is the most natural thing in the world for a Christian colleague, as well as a Christian boss, to want to pass on to others what he knows in his heart and experience to be the only way of life. But very often we forget that the spoken word is only one of the many forms of witness. We are in intimate contact day by day over a number of years with virtually the same colleagues and subordinates; over that time action speaks a good deal louder than words, and qualities of character are known as minutely as if they were charted on office walls. Our energy and single-mindedness at work, our cheerfulness under strain, our firmness in a crisis, our fairness in conduct, our helpfulness in trouble, our concern for those around us—all these are noticed and memorized; anything we say will always be correlated with the way in which we behave.

Of course, what we do is not the only effective carrier for our witness to the absolute exclusion of what we say. What we say has its place. A flaunting of our faith on every conceivable and inconceivable occasion is wrong. What we say has to be natural to us and to the occasion. But a Christian ought to be in a position to take advantage of the occasion when it arises. The apostle Peter tells us, "Always be prepared to make a defense to anyone who calls you to account for the hope that is in you, yet do it with gentleness and reverence." Not, it may be noted, with "bounce and self-confidence." However, our statement of faith should not be an indiscriminate "pearl before swine." While we will not want to limit our conversation to close friends, detailed declarations of faith will probably be to those who are really our friends. People should feel that our friendship is not a means to an end, even if that end is their conversion to the faith. Our friendship should be both natural and genuine and intended to last. Humanly speaking, one real friendship is more likely to lead to conversion than a score of declarations to those we scarcely know.

While every Christian will hope for occasions when he can say something of his faith, he should remember that he may achieve more in the long run by bringing his friends to church. He should also remember that a moral life is not enough. There are many philosophies of moral life. A Christian is different from a Mormon, however much their moralities might agree at particular points. The difference should be seen, but it should also in some way be pointed out; it is often seen more clearly in the context of a Christian church and its teaching than it can be seen just by acquaintance and conversation with individual Christians.

We are perhaps advocating a much higher degree of sensitivity on the part of the Christian to the man of the world than the latter is prepared to concede in return. The man of the world is not slow to justify his actions or to attack the standards of those he thinks are being too particular. But he is not illogical in expecting better standards from a Christian, and a Christian should remember that his standards are absolute and not relative. Above all, a Christian should be sensitive to others, and they should be aware of a real sympathy and understanding on his part.

THE PLACE OF CHRISTIAN SERVICE

Many Christians find that one of their greatest problems in relation to their work is the conflicting demands of their work and their part-time Christian activities. Some feel that the church is now so weak that the layperson has to play a much more active part. Unfortunately a minority take this so far that they are content to do an "adequate" day's work only, to leave their real energies free for external activities, particularly Christian activities. This kind of mental working to rule may be justified in routine work, but is an attitude that is not really compatible with most responsible jobs. A Christian's witness in his work is vital. People judge our profession of faith on our behavior on the job and particularly on our attitude when the going is tough. People at work with a Christian tend to regard his preoccupation with church activities as no more justifiable than preoccupation with a hobby. Whatever we do, we should be able to put our hearts into it, and we cannot conscientiously take on involvement in outside activity that requires that we are less involved in the job than the demands of the job require.

This problem mainly applies to those who could obtain promotion. There are certainly examples of people who have deliberately forsworn promotion to positions of responsibility and have remained in the lower regions of the civil service or banking or in routine university posts in order to fulfill a specialized calling in Christian service and, in some cases, this calling has been very worthwhile for the church. In times and places where the full-time ministry of the church is inadequate, God may call someone in this way. But to agree to these exceptions does not invalidate the principle, and damage is done if these situations are not regarded as being exceptional. At the other extreme, of course, we must not allow our jobs to run away with us. A ruthlessly single-minded pursuit of our job to the exclusion of church and family life is an equal error in the other direction.

There are some organizations that press strongly for an almost feudal loyalty from their employees. This poses problems for any intelligent and independently minded employee, but especially for a Christian. A Christian should, as we said in a previous chapter, have the highest standard of work and workmanship, and he owes a professional loyalty to these standards. In addition, he owes a loyalty to the people who employ him. It is when these two loyalties come into conflict that he is sometimes troubled.

Loyalty to an employer does not consist in being a yes-man. Those who under pressure say that a project can be done for half the price, even though their professional experience tells them that it cannot, are doing the greatest disservice to their firm. Loyalty consists in the duty of care which someone who is paid by a company owes to the interests of that company as against the world at large. He must take care that his own company's interests are not damaged. This duty of care is still the same even when he has decided to leave and is being interviewed for a position in another firm. In this case he must not divulge anything to his prospective employer that would not be in his firm's best interests. Indiscretions at interviews are unfortunately notorious. Even after he has left he has some loyalty to his previous employer and colleagues. Our attitude toward the firm in public should be one of respect. To criticize openly is almost certain to harm the interests of the company, and it is a good general principle that it does no good to wash one's dirty linen in public.

Loyalty, however, must not be blind. The mystique of loyalty that might be appropriate to government or to family (both of which are divinely ordained institutions) or that may be thought necessary in an army (where discipline is a matter of life or death) is quite inappropriate to a commercial enterprise—which is neither divinely ordained nor involved directly in matters of life and death. Relationship with an employer in a free society is contractual. Allegiance to a business should not involve the equivalent of oaths or declarations of loyalty, and it is quite wrong for employers to demand them. This kind of attitude is most common in family businesses, but in very large corporations, where consistent success and high standards of craftsmanship or professional expertise has produced a corporate *élan,* there is a temptation to pursue the cult of the firm as an institution. This is all right up to a point, but care has to be taken to see that it does not get out of hand. Provided the corporate tradition encourages a continuance of high standards, it is useful; but it should never become an end in itself. There is a proper sense of pride in belonging to the management of a company that is in the forefront of its industry—the kind of pride associated with belonging to a crack regiment. Yet too often, in a swiftly changing world, the tradition becomes more important than the reality, and at this point it can begin to do harm by blinding management to the facts of life. True loyalty will do its best for the company by trying to improve it, not by pretending not to notice its faults.

CHANGING JOBS

From a practical point of view the most important decision most people have to make involving principles of loyalty is when they begin to wonder whether they should change jobs. A Christian will be less likely to want to leave the company if he has been careful in choosing his company in the first place. He will not want to spend his time and talent on a business that does not have some positive social usefulness. He will want to be able to be enthusiastic and not apologetic about his work. He will want to beware particularly of going into an industry or profession because it has acquired a temporary glamor or is, for the moment, considered smart. If, for instance, he goes into advertising or television he should do so because he has real talents in this direction and not because they are more acceptable socially than other activities that are less in the public eye. We should try to find out as much as we can about the company we are thinking of joining: What sort of people does it employ? (Good employers usually attract good employees.) Has it a reputation for fair dealing in the industry? Are its labor relations enlightened? Is it really making a contribution to the social and economic life of the country? Is there a challenge in the job? What opportunities are there for the individual to make a real contribution?

Those who are at the beginning of their business career have to be particularly careful, because it is invaluable to have high standards both of ethics and competence in one's initial training. They should not only look at the company's training program to make certain that it is thorough and realistic and practical, but it would also be useful to look at the position of ex-trainees in the company. In addition, the company's financial results give a general guide as to its competence. No employer is perfect, and it would be foolish to expect to find everything so. But there is a vast difference between the standards of work and the ideals of different companies.

If we do finally decide to leave a company, what principles should guide us? As a rule of thumb most people agree that no one should leave before he puts into the firm as much as he has taken out. This applies particularly to those who change from the company in which they have been trained. A Christian may well feel justified in changing if he feels that his present company is not using his experience to the full or if, for instance, it is obvious that it cannot afford to pay salaries comparable to other firms in the industry. On the other hand, he should not try to exploit his training and experience at the expense of the firm from which he has gained it. The electronics industry in the U.S. has numerous cases of scientists who have walked out *en bloc* and made their fortunes by gaining contracts at the expense of their old firms, who were left high and dry.

A Christian should have a good reason for leaving before he has served a reasonable period in any one firm. What is reasonable should depend on the industry and the immediate situation in the firm. He owes it to the company also, when he does go, to leave a well-organized situation behind so that he minimizes any damage caused by his departure.

A Christian might well have it as his objective to make a contribution at the highest level of his ability in any organization that is itself making an outstanding contribution to society. If he can do this, he will probably find that he has solved not only the problem of loyalty, but a good many other problems as well.

It is right to look at these problems of the individual Christian in a secular industrial organization and to put forward some principles on which they might be solved. But it would be quite wrong to leave the impression that any one Christian would encounter all these problems or indeed that those he did encounter would arise with any frequency. Nor do these problems arise only in industrial organizations.

Industrial society—at any rate in Britain and America—has the merit of being fairly open; it is easier to move around to find congenial work and company than it is in some of the narrower professional hierarchies. But more important, there are a great many individual companies with very fine standards and traditions, which a Christian can accept without hesitation and which he himself can help to support and strengthen. There may be much that is wrong in industrial life, but there is much good too. It is on this that we in our own generation must build.

Conclusion

In this book an attempt has been made to draw on the experience of Christians working in industry and commerce and to set down the outcome of a number of discussions on problems that arise in everyday life, in the hope that this may be of some help to those who are setting out to earn their living in this way.

But the Christian standard is so high and the complexities of modern business so great that none of those associated with the preparation of this book would claim for a moment either that all the opinions expressed in it are in any sense infallible or that they themselves have succeeded or do always succeed in putting into effect the principles set out.

However, if the book has drawn attention to the fact that Christianity is relevant to the problems of everyday life in industry and commerce and that, however falteringly he may do so, the Christian has a part to play in it, then it will have served a useful purpose.

Ultimately we all have to decide for ourselves how we should act in any situation. In coming to a decision, a Christian should never forget that the principles of his faith are a most relevant and important factor.

Appendix

THE WEBER-TAWNEY THESIS

ANY CONTEMPORARY discussion of the relation between the Christian faith and work must of necessity draw upon a great deal of thought about industrial society that has gone on in the twentieth century. This is all the more needful because of the author's challenge to the Christian at work to build upon the good in industrial society for the sake of our own generation and future ones.

Much discussion in our century has focused on and been stirred by what has become known as the Weber-Tawney thesis. This appendix is offered in the hope that it will provide some useful background to the foregoing discussion in this book to the Christian employee or employer whose labors have been primarily in the practical rather than the theoretical side of the matter.

At the beginning of this century, the German social historian, Max Weber, made a major study entitled *The Protestant Ethic and the Spirit of Capitalism*. In Great Britain, R. H. Tawney wrote the introduction to the English translation of Weber's book and in the thirties published his own book, *Religion and the Rise of Capitalism*. Other writers have also dealt with aspects of the subject in passing, including F. A. Hayek in *Capitalism and the Historians* and Christopher Hill in *Puritanism and Revolution, The Century of Revolution,* and *Society and Puritanism in Pre-Revolutionary England*.

Weber had noted that business leaders, higher grades of skilled labor and the higher technically and commercially trained personnel in any country of mixed religions were predominantly Protestant.[1] He concluded that the underlying attitude of mind of Protestants was different. Their ethos was more dynamic than that of any preceding trading system. When this spirit took hold of some members of a trade that had been carried on with a traditional rate of profit and a traditional rate of

[1]*The Protestant Ethic and the Spirit of Capitalism* (English translation, 1930), p. 35.

work, the "leisureliness was suddenly destroyed . . . the idyllic state collapsed" and "gave way to a hard frugality in which some came to the top because they did not wish to consume but to earn."[2] The men who carried through this change had "grown up in the hard school of life, calculating and daring at the same time, above all temperate and reliable, shrewd and completely devoted to their business."[3]

Weber looked for the background to the ideas of this new generation and found it in the Protestant conception of "calling," a conception unknown among either Catholic peoples or in classical antiquity. "The idea of calling is a product of the Reformation and one thing was unquestionably new. The valuation of the fulfilment of duty in worldly affairs as the highest form of moral activity."[4] To Luther, "labour in a calling appears as the outward expression of brotherly love" in contrast with monasticism's selfish renunciation of temporal obligations.[5] Weber contrasts the Protestant attitude with the "hand-to-mouth existence of the peasant; the privileged traditionalism of the guild craftsman; adventurer's capitalism, oriented to exploitation of political opportunities and irrational speculation."[6] He concludes that "the restraints which were made upon the consumption of wealth" made possible the "productive investment of capital."[7]

Going deeper into the theological basis of the "calling," Weber says that the Protestant identifies true faith by objective results, by conduct that serves to increase the glory of God. Conviction of his own salvation cannot, "as in Catholicism, consist in a gradual accumulation of good works to one's credit, but rather in a systematic self-control."[8] God demanded "not single good works but a life of good works combined into a unified system. There was no place for the very human Catholic cycle of sin, repentance, atonement and release, followed by renewed sin."[9] Weber regarded his works as no more than a preliminary study, but unfortunately he died before completing the task he had set himself.

Tawney's book was written in the thirties as a political challenge to

---

[2]Ibid., pp. 67–68.

[3]Ibid., p. 69.

[4]Ibid., p. 60.

[5]Ibid., p. 61.

[6]Ibid., p. 76.

[7]Ibid., p. 172.

[8]Ibid., p. 115.

[9]Ibid., p. 117.

laissez-faire economics and as an appeal for a morality in economic life to replace the morality that the church had once tried to impose. The early Protestant church leaders had tried to maintain a moral code in business affairs, but the economic explosion, produced in some degree by their own ethic, had so enlarged and diversified economic life that the sort of control which the medieval church had tried to exercise on the simpler business life of its day was no longer possible. Trade became increasingly secularized until finally, in the nineteenth century, utility was put forward as the sole guide to action. Tawney is most interesting in describing the kind of men who, in his view, created this explosive change.

The enemy of Calvinism "is not the accumulation of riches, but their misuse for purposes of self-indulgence or ostentation."[10] Calvinism "is intensely practical. Good works are not a way of attaining salvation, but they are indispensable as proof that salvation has been attained."[11] "Compared with the quarrelsome self-indulgent nobility of most European countries . . . the middle classes, in whom Calvinism took root most deeply, were a race of iron. It was not surprising that they made several revolutions and imprinted their conceptions of political and social expediency on the public life of half a dozen different states in the Old World and in the New."[12]

The Puritan "has within himself a principle at once of energy and of order which makes him irresistible, both in war and in the struggles of commerce."[13] In society "Puritanism worked like the yeast which sets the whole mass fermenting."[14] The conception that sprang from the very heart of Puritan theology was the "calling." "The rational order of the universe is the work of God and its plan requires that the individual should labour for God's glory."[15]

The labor of the Puritan moralist "is not merely an economic means to be laid aside when physical needs have been satisfied. It is a spiritual end and must be continued as an ethical duty, long after it has ceased to be a material necessity."[16] The idea of economic progress as an end to be consciously sought . . . had been unfamiliar to most earlier

---

[10]*Religion and the Rise of Capitalism* (Pelican, 1930), p. 114.

[11]Ibid., p. 117.

[12]Ibid., p. 120.

[13]Ibid., p. 229.

[14]Ibid., p. 230.

[15]Ibid., p. 239.

[16]Ibid., p. 240.

generations of Englishmen. . . . It found a new sanction in the identification of labour and enterprise with the service of God. The magnificent energy which changed in a century the face of material civilization was to draw nourishment from that temper."[17]

Neither Weber nor Tawney is saying that the Protestant ethic advocated laissez-faire capitalism or can, in any way, be identified with it. The kind of utilitarian philosophy which says that "What is good for General Motors is good for America" came two or three centuries later and was propounded by men who made no particular profession of Christianity. V. H. H. Green, Fellow of Lincoln College, Oxford, deals with this point in an appendix to *Renaissance and Reformation.* He concludes that "the Reformation did not cause, or even encourage, except incidentally, the development of capitalism; Protestants and Catholics remained very suspicious of unethical business enterprise, such as capitalism undoubtedly stimulated. Nevertheless, Protestantism (even more than Catholicism) may have done much, even in its early days, to stimulate efficiency and success in business. . . . It should be remembered that capitalism did not emerge as a dominant force until the nineteenth century. By that time religious sanctions had so weakened that the church's approval was remembered after its significant moral qualifications had been largely forgotten."[18]

A SENSE OF PURPOSE

F. A. Hayek was concerned in *Capitalism and the Historians* with the easy acceptance by historians and economists, from Marx onward, of the view that growth of wealth was at the expense of a hitherto happy proletariat. "It was only when the larger gains, from the employment of machinery, provided both the means and the opportunity for their investment that what had been in the past a recurring surplus of population doomed to early death was in an increasing measure given the possibility of survival."[19] "The very increase of wealth and well-being which had been achieved raised standards and aspirations. What for ages had seemed a natural and inevitable situation . . . came to be regarded as incongruous. . . . Economic suffering both became more conspicuous and seemed less justified, because the general wealth was increasing faster than ever before."[20]

---

[17]Ibid., p. 247.

[18]*Renaissance and Reformation* (1952), pp. 400–401.

[19]*Capitalism and the Historians,* Introductory Essay by F. A. Hayek (1954), p. 16.

[20]Ibid., p. 18.

An important contribution to the subject was made by Christopher Hill, Master of Balliol College, Oxford. In *The Century of Revolution,* he says, "Calvinism liberated those who believed themselves to be the elect from a sense of sin, of helplessness; it encouraged effort, industry, study, a sense of purpose. It prepared the way for modern science. . . . The Puritan preachers insisted that the universe was law-abiding. . . . It was man's duty to study the universe and find out its laws. . . . Bacon called men to study the world about them. . . . The end of knowledge was 'the relief of man's estate,' 'to subdue and overcome the necessities and miseries of humanity.' Acceptance of this novel doctrine constituted the greatest intellectual revolution of the century."[21]

Hill has also contributed an essay on "Protestantism and the Rise of Capitalism" to *Essays in the Economic and Social History of Tudor and Stuart England.* He begins by saying, "Most historians would now accept the existence of some connection between protestantism and the rise of capitalism, though Professor [H. R.] Trevor-Roper is a conspicuous exception." "The central target of the Reformers' attack was justification by works. . . . The Protestant objection was to mechanical actions in which the heart was not involved . . . a Protestant thought that what a man did was less important than the spirit in which he did it. . . . For Christians no action can be casual or perfunctory, the most trivial detail of our daily life should be performed to the glory of God; should be irradiated with a conscious co-operation with God's purposes."[22] "It was in fact the labour of generations of God-fearing Puritans that made England the leading industrial nation in the world."[23]

In *The Intellectual Origins of the English Revolution,* Hill looks at the connection between the Puritans, the Parliamentarians, and science,[24] and in his study of Francis Bacon finds all three closely interwoven. Bacon wanted the advance of science by planning and direction, not by "blind and stupid" methods which were "more like 'a kind of hunting by scent than a science.'"[25] "The further discovering of knowledge" was part of God's plan, and "scientific investigation not only did not conflict with divinity but was positively virtuous."[26]

---

[21]*The Century of Revolution 1603–1714* (1961), pp. 92–94.

[22]F. J. Fisher (ed.), *Essays in the Economic and Social History of Tudor and Stuart England* (1961), pp. 16–21.

[23]Ibid., p. 31.

[24]Christopher Hill, *Intellectual Origins of the English Revolution* (1965), p. 106.

[25]Ibid., pp. 86f.

[26]Ibid., p. 87.

Bacon inherited from his pious parents, and imbibed from the world around him, Calvinist assumptions about the priority of faith over reason—as well as about the necessity for strenuous effort. "All knowledge is to be limited by religion." "If any man shall think by view and enquiry into these sensible and material things, to attain to any light for the revealing of the nature or the will of God; he shall dangerously abuse himself. Approaching and intruding into God's secrets and mysteries" was the cause of the Fall. . . . "Let us never think or maintain that a man can search too far . . . in the book of God's word or in the book of God's works . . . but . . . let men beware . . . that they do not unwisely mingle or confound these learnings together."[27]

"This subsumes a long trend in Protestant thought, from Luther onwards, which equated charity with works done with intent to benefit the commonwealth or mankind; and so Bacon's separation of science from religion, so vital for the future advance of science, was in the best Protestant tradition." "Bacon gave the scientists' activities a moral sanction. . . . Religion . . . instead of opposing science 'should clearly protect all increase in natural knowledge.'" "Bacon was not separating religion and science because he was a secret atheist. . . . The separation sprang from his Protestant beliefs. . . . Calvin himself assumed the importance of final and formal causes and gave unusual significance to material and efficient causes."[28]

"Bacon's emphasis on secondary causes . . . fortified and gave deeper significance to the Parliamentarian preference for the rule of law against arbitrariness. A similar emphasis on the law-abiding nature of the universe can be seen in the dominant school of Puritan theologians under Charles I, Preston and Ames. The new science, moreover, combined respect for law with a willingness to innovate."[29] "If Professor Butterfield is right to regard the emergence of a new scientific civilization in the later seventeenth century as the greatest landmark since the rise of Christianity, then so far as England is concerned Bacon is clearly the decisive figure."[30]

THE SCIENTIFIC BREAKTHROUGH

Herbert Butterfield takes the view in *The Origins of Modern Science* that, although there was no continuity from the ancients through

[27]Ibid., p. 91.
[28]Ibid., pp. 92f.
[29]Ibid., pp. 109f.
[30]Ibid., p. 111.

the Renaissance to the moderns, "we cannot say that essentially new ingredients were introduced into our civilization at the Renaissance."[31] In his view, the real breakthrough came in the seventeenth century, which "represents one of the great episodes in human experience which ought to be placed among the epic adventures that have helped to make the human race what it is. It represents one of those periods when new things are brought into the world and into history out of men's own creative activity."[32]

This scientific movement "was localized and it is connected with the humming activity which was taking place, say from 1660, not only in England, Holland and France, but actually between these countries."[33] "Not only did England and Holland hold a leading position, but that part of France which was most active in promoting the new order was the Huguenot section."[34] After the revocation of the Edict of Nantes in 1685, the Huguenots in exile played a key part; as the pattern crystallized, "it was the northern half of the continent that came to the forefront and it was soon decided that this northern part should be British, not French, Protestant, not Roman Catholic—an ally, therefore, of the new form of civilization."[35]

It is perhaps relevant at this point to look at the economic position today of individual Protestant countries and to compare them with the countries that have a different religion and culture. We find that there is a fairly clear pattern. Taking income per capita of population as the best indication of national wealth, seven Protestant countries—Switzerland, Sweden, the United States of America, Denmark, Germany, Canada, and Norway—come at the head of the list. They are followed by the other countries of the European Community, Protestant and Catholic, with the remaining Protestant countries Australia, Finland, and New Zealand. Italy and Ireland, both Catholic countries, tail this group. It also includes two rich countries outside the Christian culture, Japan and Israel. Israel has a parallel culture based on the Old Testament, but it is also a very small country heavily dependent on external aid, especially from the United States.

Japan is the most significant exception to the general rule. It is, as has been mentioned, a highly disciplined society. But it owes a great

---

[31] *The Origins of Modern Science 1300–1800* (1957), p. 178.

[32] Ibid., p. 179.

[33] Ibid., p. 180.

[34] Ibid., p. 181.

[35] Ibid.

deal to its close alliance since World War II with the United States, which brought postwar financial aid, a very generous trading partnership, and relief from all defense expenditure. The European Community does not feel that the Japanese will have been put to the test until they can import the same proportion of foreign manufactured goods as other industrial nations. Nor is Japan's income as high as it seems, for it is badly housed and its social infrastructure is primitive compared with other countries with a similar income. But with those qualifications, Japan is still a remarkable exception.

Greece, Spain, East Germany, Poland, and the Soviet Union have incomes per capita about half that of the European Community. East Germany claims a higher income, but it is hard to judge the income in Communist countries, since they have an artificial exchange rate. Venezuela and Argentina also fall into this group as two rich South American countries, with the most of South America at about a quarter of the European Community rate, which they share with the poorer Communist countries of Eastern Europe.

Excluding the oil states for obvious reasons, the non-Christian countries are led by the small, talented Chinese expatriate communities in Hong Kong and Singapore, who have about half the European Community standard of living. These are followed at a great distance by the majority of other non-Christian countries. India's income per capita is only 3 percent of the average of the European Community, Egypt's is 6 percent, Burma's 2 percent.

So the real gulf is not between Protestant and Catholic, or Protestant and Orthodox, but between the countries with a Christian culture and the average country with a non-Christian culture. Even the Communist countries seem to owe a great deal more to their long cultural history. It has been said that only the Germans can make communism work—to which the East Germans reply that only the Germans can make capitalism work. The answer in both cases may be that the Protestant ethic makes any system work better.

The classification is governed by the religion predominating during the main period of economic growth of the country. In most cases this does not differ substantially from the religious affiliation given in the latest censuses. In some countries the Catholic population has grown substantially in the last twenty or thirty years. Even so, in the United States there are still 3 Protestants to every 2 Catholics, in Australia 3 to 1, in Switzerland 4 to 3. In the Netherlands, the Catholics are now almost equal in numbers, and in Canada the Protestants are in a bare majority. (However, excluding Quebec, which has a lower per capita income, the Protestants are 2 to 1.) In West Germany there are 10 Protestants to 9 Catholics, but before the division of the country the ratio was nearer 3 to 2.

REASONS FOR PROSPERITY

Two explanations are put forward for the exceptional prosperity of the Protestant countries. One is that it is the effect of a temperate climate. This does not really bear examination. The U.S. and Australia are both countries with extremes of climate, and both are exceptionally prosperous. Eire and Denmark have almost identical climates, products, populations, and resources, but the Danish income is twice that of Eire. The natural resources and climates of North America and South America are not so dissimilar and both were settled by Europeans, but one is prosperous and developed and the other is poor and underdeveloped. Within countries, the Protestants are usually more prosperous than the Catholics. This is true of Canada, Switzerland, and Ireland.

The other commonly held view is that the characteristics which lead people to work hard also lead them to adopt the Protestant faith. Although this sounds like a reasonable view for those who do not accept Christian teaching, it is quite contrary to that teaching. We are told that the faith is for all and that "there is neither Jew nor Greek, . . . bond nor free." A sovereign God cannot be limited by such trifles as national or social characteristics. But even from the secular point of view, the argument does not hold. There is no evidence that before the Reformation the Swedes, the Scots, or the Pomeranians were more hardworking and prosperous than the Italians, the Spaniards, or the French. On the contrary, southern Europe was much more advanced than northern Europe. The converts of Whitefield and the Wesleys were mainly from the hitherto improvident working class. In the last hundred years the Christian faith has been accepted by members of every race in ever-increasing numbers. The facts do not support the argument that certain social or racial types respond more readily to the Christian faith.

Various other factors affect the prosperity of countries. War has a temporary effect, as does the possession of natural resources in current demand. However, it is noticeable that some of the most prosperous countries have scarcely any natural resources. This is particularly true of Switzerland and Holland; and the natural resources of others, such as New Zealand and Denmark, are limited.

But whatever the differences between Protestant and Catholic, the countries with real poverty are those that until recently were right outside any Christian influence. It may be that the colonial powers did not promote the economies of their former colonies as vigorously as they might, but surely some of this poverty arises from an inherited attitude toward life, though this may now have been largely repudiated by their leaders.

The extensive and complex organization of industry (for low-cost production and distribution) is common to communist, socialist, and capitalist countries. But where it does not have the backing of the state, industry must operate without any form of compulsion or sanction in dealing with its workers, suppliers, and customers and it must attract workers, customers, and capital in the open market against the offers of other similar organizations. Large and independent industrial organizations of today's size and complexity have not existed before this century. The extent to which they should, or even can, be made democratically answerable is one of the major political questions of our time; but their success in the past in raising living standards and providing the governments with tax revenue on an unprecedented scale is not in question.

The interesting point for us is that it does not seem to have been possible for these organizations to grow on any scale in other than Protestant countries. Elsewhere, organization of this size seems to need military or feudal sanctions and docile labor; or monopoly powers and docile customers; or strong doses of expatriate capital and management; or they need the cream of a country's talent, so that the country cannot sustain more than one or two such organizations. This may not always be so, if only because it is easier to copy than to initiate, but until now only the Protestants have seemed to want both freedom and economic development enough to impose on themselves the disciplines required to achieve both a free economy and the economies of scale. These disciplines are now breaking up and with them the viability of companies.

There is evidence for the view that the strength or weakness of management too would seem to be related to whether a country is Protestant or not. Studies published in 1959 by Harbison of Princeton and C. A. Myers of the Massachusetts Institute of Technology, under the title *Management in the Industrial World,* compared the quality of industrial management in the U.S., the United Kingdom, Sweden, Germany, France, Italy, Egypt, India, Chile, and Japan. The first four all appear to have achieved a high standard of industrial management on a fairly wide scale and have, of course, a high standard of living.

Standards of management among the others are reported to be much poorer and, with the exception of France, they all have a much lower standard of living.

These weaknesses in management seem to run to a pattern in all the non-Protestant countries and are traceable directly to ethical causes. Managers are gravely concerned with their authority and the preservation of their prerogatives. They prefer docile employees "who will not talk back or raise questions" rather than employees who are ambitious or efficient.[36] Typical organizational structure is highly centralized and personal. There is little delegation and consequently much frustration and bitterness on the part of subordinate managers.[37] Key positions are occupied by family members on the basis of family ties and not on the basis of performance.[38] The family is more important than the enterprise. Maximum production and performance have little place in the family plans.[39] "The end supreme and all pervading, is the family—its economic security, its social prestige."[40] The object of the business is to provide a reasonable degree of wealth for the family, and it is not felt that the productivity of the enterprise need be pushed beyond this point. All this contrasts sharply with management philosophy in the U.S. or the U.K., where it is generally held to be intolerable that personal interests should stand in the way of a major enterprise responsible for the employment and standard of living of thousands of workers.

FALSE CONCLUSIONS

It would be quite wrong to draw from these limited findings any conclusions of racial superiority or inferiority. The Protestant ethic is clearly a waning force in a country in which the Christian faith no longer has any influence. Humanism, the prevailing faith in many of the countries that are still nominally Protestant, may have taken over many of the ethical ideals of Christianity, but it remains to be seen whether, having taken away the theology (the "why" of religion), the ethic (the "what" of religion) will retain its grip.

Only now are we encountering the third generation since the major decline of church-going. If the Christian faith ceased to have any influence in Northern Europe but took a firm grip in, say, Brazil, which

[36]*Management in the Industrial World* (1959), p. 164.

[37]Ibid., p. 143.

[38]Ibid., pp. 148, 236.

[39]Ibid., p. 171.

[40]Ibid., p. 247.

has a growing Protestant minority, then the relative patterns of national prosperity and growth might change quite decisively over a relatively short period. It is unfortunately all too easy to imagine the deterioration that could set in here if management and labor increasingly took their tone from their worst elements. Nor is it so very difficult to imagine the results of a full exploitation of the considerable natural resources of Brazil.

It would also be quite naïve to use these findings as an argument for laissez-faire capitalism and against, for instance, state socialism. Socialism may or may not be able to produce comparable prosperity—it is to early to say. If it does succeed, it will probably be for different reasons, although non-Communist socialism does appear to require an even higher ethic than capitalism for its success. But the argument between communism, socialism, and capitalism and their variations should not turn, for a Christian, on prosperity alone. The freedom of the individual is an even more important consideration. Capitalism may or may not be an unintended by-product of the Protestant ethic, but the ethic is much broader than capitalism or socialism and not to be confined to either.

Nor should we conclude too much from the difference between Protestants and Catholics. A Catholic, particularly one educated and living in a Protestant country, can be an example to many a Protestant in his standards of work and professional integrity. And deeply though we must disagree with our Catholic friends on the doctrines of justification and the church, we can hardly be further from them than we are from those so-called Protestants who deny the deity of Christ and whose concept of Christian authority is absolutely minimal. And the really dramatic and unarguable difference is not between Protestant and Catholic, but between these two and the non-Christian religions.

Above all it would be wrong to draw the conclusion that we should be Christians in order to be prosperous. There is no promise in the Bible that all Christians will be prosperous in this life. They may be persecuted, exiled, despoiled, and oppressed for their faith. Indeed, this is all too often the position of Christian minorities. It is only where there is fairly widespread acceptance of the Christian ethic combined with freedom from war and civil unrest that a Christian's way of life can begin to produce greater prosperity for himself and for those with whom he lives. Even so, individual Christians may not share in the benefits and may see the rewards of their labor go elsewhere.

What does seem fairly clear is that Protestant Christianity has provided a necessary element in what was, and as a rule still is, needed to encourage the development of science, commerce, and industry. This does not imply that all those concerned were more than nominal Christians, but only that they had a certain attitude toward work that derived from the Christian faith and was not found elsewhere. It is likely, however, that in its beginnings in any community the Protestant ethic was promoted by those who were sincere and deeply committed Christians.

E. G. Rupp summed up this whole question in an article in *The Times* of London in 1964 on the anniversary of Calvin's death. "So far from belief in predestination breeding an enervating fatalism," he wrote, "it rather engendered a robust taste for liberty, a race of free men, a crop of free institutions in one country after another, in Holland, Scotland, France and in the New World. That Calvin's teaching has some direct relation to the rise of Capitalism is a thesis more than a little damaged. But it is true that Calvin's doctrine of vocation is, more than Luther's, apt for a citizen in a world of trade and commerce, and if it is Bucer who is the father of the 'Gospel of hard work,' Calvin too insisted on the virtues of thrift and diligence, duty and responsibility. Without ever going back on the great watchword 'By Faith alone,' the characteristic theme for the Calvinist Christian is that he lives by faith, for the honour and service of God in a world the whole life of which must be brought from sinful chaos into the ordered liberty of the children of God."

Subject Index

Scripture Index